MYU

First Printing, 2015

ISBN 978-1-326-23975-6

www.makeyourselfuncomfortable.net

Make Yourself Uncomfortable

Ron Gridcharts (anag.)

Dear Nick.

Been a pleasure "working" with you. Don't stay in the Gulf too long... time it is a-flying!

All the best

Rick AKA Ron

9/8/15

About the Author

Ron Gridcharts is a cunning anagram. Born in 1973, he has spent.

You can follow Ron Gridcharts. If he turns around, though, it's best to pretend you are reading a newspaper or are checking out the bus timetable or something.

www.makeyourselfuncomfortable.net
Twitter: @rongridcharts

Well, there's a turnip for the books.
makeyourselfuncomfortable.net

Oh yeah, just a heads up:

PARENTAL

ADVISORY

EXPLICIT CONTENT

Table of Contents

When I was seventeen, my father decided that we would move from the flat above his town centre pub in Stratford-Upon-Avon to a thatched cottage in a hamlet called Wixford.

"It's our Magic Cottage," he said, indicating his second wife, a chancer from East London who was pretending to be a conceptual artist. "Just like that James Herbert book."

The fact that James Herbert is known as 'the British Stephen King', only with extra perviness, did little to convince me that my family were making anything other than a massive lurch in the wrong direction.

"It's got two fireplaces," my Welsh grandmother had said, disapprovingly. "That's a bad omen, that is. You'll have nothing but trouble."

The cottage was five or six hundred years old, thatched and stuck on a main road where juggernauts thundered past in the early hours, its lead-lined windows with their original tiny panes offering very little sound protection.

As we were on the main road, curious passers by would sometimes peer in through the tiny windows.

"Have a good fucking look, why don't you!" my father would bellow at them from the sofa, their startled faces registering shock and dismay at the ogre whose cottage this was.

\- - -

It wasn't long after we moved in that we realised the place was haunted and whatever the presence was, it wasn't entirely friendly.

My sister noticed it first as it centred itself on her bedroom, across the landing from my own. She was watching a horror film on TV when she felt the bed covers start moving. The bedroom light started flickering also.

A few days later, my father and his wife went away for the weekend.

On the Sunday morning, my sister woke me up, calling for me from the living room.

"Rick! Rick! Come and look at this- oh my God."

I got out of bed about as quickly as is possible for a seventeen-year-old (i.e. not that quickly at all) and went down the stairs, wondering what could possibly have happened.

"Look at the curtains!" she was saying, a horrified look on her face, gesturing up at the curtain rail.

"Are you tripping or something?" I asked. It was a reasonable question. She was doing a lot of clubbing at the time.

"No, no- really LOOK at the CURTAINS," she repeated.

I shook my head, sadly. Another victim of rave culture.

It was only when she pulled on the curtains to close them that I realised she wasn't being leader of the lost-it posse at all. In fact, the curtain rings had been somehow removed and replaced on the outside of the curtain rail stoppers, so that the curtains could no longer be closed at all. This had happened in the night when we were both asleep and for sure nobody had been in the house except us: the back door was chained and the front bolted.

"Whoa. That's pretty scary."

My sister moved out soon after, going to live with some friends back in Stratford. I didn't see much of her for a while.

- – -

My father was sad to see her go of course, being a control freak, but happy that there was now a spare room for guests.

But it was an undeniable fact that many of these guests reported strange and unwelcome occurrences in the night: the sensation of someone sleeping in the bed next to them; the sound of breathing; the lights not working.

A school friend who came to stay claimed he had been picked up and thrown violently out of the bed. He refused to ever stay again.

My grandmother, equal parts psychic and psycho, claimed it was an old woman who had owned the cottage many years- possibly centuries- before. She said she had felt her physical form manifest next to her when she stayed one night.

My father breezily brushed aside all the troubling aspects of there being an unquiet spirit in the house. "Isn't it great that we've got a ghost?" he'd exclaim. "It makes me feel safer, if anything!" He had always had an affinity for spirits, of course: mainly vodka and rum.

One evening, however, he was sat on the postage stamp-sized lawn out the back, enjoying a finger or four of Stolichnaya, when he saw the top half of a shadowy figure cross the bottom of the garden and disappear behind the newly-built garage.

"Well, we'll just have to learn to share, I suppose" he eventually said, but you could tell he was freaked out about it.

- – -

Although not a supernatural occurrence, one night I was nearly killed when a flatbed gypsy lorry slowly trundled through the hamlet, the lads on the back casually firing metal balls from catapults through the windows of all the Wixford homes. I was going into the kitchen for something when I felt and heard the pellet buzz right past my ear before smashing through the glass of a painting on the wall.

- – -

After we had been there a few months, my father announced that he and his wife were going away for two weeks and that I was to housesit. I hadn't been on my own for a period of time like this before and particularly not in such a spooky place.

Being from a broken home, I was something of a teenage horror aficionado and so had had prior experience of bad omens. Omen III, in particular, was dreadful.

I had actually rented out the VHS of Evil Dead II over thirty times at the age of thirteen, back when video stores didn't care much about the age of their customers. It is a joyous hoot of a movie and one of my favourite films of this period.

Then came the rerelease of the original Evil Dead on home VHS (i.e. 10 quid for the tape), after having been banned since 1985 in the UK. This coincided with my father and his wife's holiday. And despite all my instincts telling me it was a foolish thing to buy when I was staying in such a spooky place on my own, when I saw it on sale in WHSmith, I simply couldn't help myself.

- – -

In comparison to the second Evil Dead, the first tries hard to be scary and, despite the special effects being made of stop-motion Plasticine in places, Sam Raimi effectively conjures up a sense of dread and foreboding. Particularly if you're a teenager alone in a demonstrably haunted ancient thatched cottage in the middle of nowhere.

- – -

Although I managed to go to sleep after watching it okay, despite being a bit scared, I was woken in the middle of the night by a thumping sound on the stairs outside my bedroom door.

I lay there for a while, praying that I didn't hear anything else. But of course I did.

Another thump.

Then a slithering kind of sound, followed by a louder thump, this time downstairs.

I could hear footsteps coming from the dining room directly below my bedroom and figured I had to investigate, although naturally I was fairly terrified.

I turned on my bedroom light and opened the door a little. Outside, the landing light had been turned on. I knew I had definitely switched everything off when I had gone to bed.

I opened the door further.

The door to my sister's old bedroom was wide open, all its lights on. The light on the stairs was on. The door at the bottom of the stairs was open and all the lights were on downstairs.

I could still hear footsteps.

I decided I had to confront whatever it was, so walked downstairs with some trepidation, but mainly anger: anger that I had been woken up; anger at my father for leaving me here with this thing; and a large dose of anger for having been forced to move to this cottage in the middle of nowhere just at a time when all my friends were busy doing all those exciting late-teen activities (underage drinking on Shottery Fields;

hanging around Bell Court; molesting grammar school girls at the Brass Rubbing Centre; that kind of thing).

The dining room was empty and the noises stopped as I entered.

"For fuck's sake!" I began "Don't you know what time it is? I've got school in the morning and YOU'VE woken me up!"

I was pointing my finger, shaking with mild rage.

"Now, get to FUCKING BED!"

At this, I felt a kind of breeze brush past me, out of the room and upstairs.

- - -

That was pretty much it for nasty manifestations as far as I was concerned, though guests still complained periodically that they felt something sleeping next to them in that room.

Regardless, and whether it was connected to my grandmother's feeling of foreboding or not, the fact remains that Bank Cottage, Wixford brought about the ruin of my father and his premature death at the age of fifty-three.

But that is another story and shall be told another time.

HANG UP YOUR COAT AND JUMP ABOARD THE
Wacky Krazyballs™
SHOW®
THIS WEEK'S STAR GUEST: SID CHADWICK THE LION
BANANAS ON TOAST! THIS IS CERTAINLY PROVING TO BE A TRICKY JOB!
DANGER DO NOT HAMMER NAILS INTO THIS
BONJOUR, WACKY! WHAT'S THE PROBLEM?
AH, SIMON! I'M TRYING TO HAMMER THIS NAIL IN USING A COMMON OR GARDEN FRUIT PASTILLE
A GREEN ONE, ACTUALLY!
ARGH! DON'T SAY THAT WORD! YOU KNOW IT MAKES ME CONVULSE!

WHAT WORD - 'GREEN'?
STOP IT, YOU FOOL! I'M GOING INTO SPASM!
QUICK! CALL ME-NNG- AN AMBULANCE!
WELL, IF YOU THINK IT'LL WORK - YOU'RE AN AMBULANCE!
DROOL

Thailand, October 2001.

I had flown into Chiang Mai from Chaweng. Three weeks of being encamped at Paradise Bungalows, Hat Rin, home of the legendary Full Moon parties, had destroyed my fragile ego. That and the thick, rich mushroom shakes I had been consuming most days at the Mountain. Every night had been a selection of techno parties on the beach and even the most ardent druggie gets tired eventually.

The final straw was at some waterfall party- a bunch of Israelis filming each other being stupid- while the tuk tuk drivers waited in a disapproving ring, their opinion of farang being lowered by the second.

Some guy called Big John had said "You can't leave now- don't you know you're fated to remain?" but he was just trying to shift me some more MDMA.

I left anyway. It seemed the thing to do.

* * *

Chaing Mai was wonderfully urban after my island sojourn. I wandered the streets and markets, checking out wooden Buddhas and wicker baskets. I ate Pad Thai at street stalls and picked up a bar girl and valium and a tourist map.

My second night I went to see some Muay Thai- Thai Boxing; sat there popping valleys and swigging Chiang. I got pissed off at some video jockeys filming proceedings for the media; made mental bets on red or blue; laughed at the music.

Each match got younger and younger till finally there were eight year olds kicking each other's heads in, fathers and uncles screaming them on.

It got uncomfortable. This was like child abuse. And besides- the diazepam was killing my blood lust.

So I left the arena, found a bridge and crossed it. Next thing was the beeping and the "Hello! Tuk tuk!"

Some guy with missing teeth was signalling me from his jalopy. "Where you going?"

"Okay. Top North," I said. "The one with the swimming pool."

"Top North? No problem."

As we drove off, he fixed me in the rear view.

"So- you want Thai lady? You want some boom boom?"

"Nah. Not really," I yawned. "I'm kind of spent."

"Okay, my friend. How about weed? You want Thai weed?"

I said something non-committal.

"You want amphetamines?"

I perked up. Maybe those pesky phets would lift me out of the valley.

"How much?"

He laughed.

"For you good price!"

Isn't it always, though?

* * *

We drove a couple of miles along a main drag then he pulled in by some food stands and told me to give him the money. He said I should maybe eat something while I waited. I wasn't crazy about this but I had come this far. I gave up my Baht and he drove away, promising to be back as soon as he could.

There was no eating for me. I had the appetite of a bulimic and had had the shits all day. I quaffed Red Bull and smoked L&Ms, waiting for his return.

After twenty minutes I got the feeling I had been ripped off, went onto the street and stared at every tuk tuk passing. Every driver shouted "Hello- need a ride?" but I was just scanning their numbers, looking for the 48. I figured I'd report him if he didn't show.

But he did show, restoring my faith in humanity, giggling like a drain and saying "Get in! Get in!"

We squealed off. He cadged a cigarette.

"Where we going?" I said, knowing we were heading away from Top North. I just wanted to score and bounce.

"We go somewhere safe," he said, then- "What's your name?"

"Rick. And yours?"

"Sunil."

"Okay."

"Where are you from?"

"England."

Now Thais normally say 'Where you from?' so this guy had a grasp of the grammar.

I said "You speak good English."

"Yeah. English lessons. Three times a week."

"Right. That's nice."

He laughed.

Down darkened side streets he took me and I started to worry. What if he had a knife? What if this was some sort of set up? I kept these fears to myself, checking to see if we were going slow enough to bail out. Being a tuk tuk driver, we weren't. So I figured go with the flow. Sometimes it's all you can do.

* * *

As we pulled up in a car port, he told me to get down on the floor of the cab. I didn't know what to think but did as I was told.

He turned off the engine, spoke to some Thai woman who was outside, then shut garage doors behind us.

"I need to lock up. Go up those stairs," he said.

I did as I was told and waited at the door at the top of them. Presently he arrived. "Go in, go in, the room's not locked."

Inside was a living room, sofa and TV blaring.

"Safe house," he said. "Many drivers use this."

I nodded. He laughed. He got out the drugs.

"Here's the amphetamines," he said, showing me seven or eight pink pills.

"Pills? What, you swallow these?" I said.

"Not swallow. Smoke."

"Wow. Is this Yaa baa?" I said.

"Yep." he laughed again.

Yaa baa. It's something you must keep quiet about in Thailand, on account of it tearing the social fabric apart. Widely reputed to be synthesised in military factories in Burma, it has created an army of addicts in Thailand some two million strong. Literally, it means 'crazy medicine' or 'horse medicine'. It can get you the death penalty.

"People take it for one, two years maybe, then-" Sunil said, making a flapping motion with his arms.

"You jump off a building?"

"Exactly."

He showed me how to smoke it. You take the silver from the cigarette paper, rip some off to form a tooter and burn the paper off the back of the rest. You pinch this into a V and place the Yaa baa in the fold then burn on a low flame from beneath. Not as unpleasant as smack, but in that ballpark.

Within ten minutes, I had pins and needles, had to start walking the room. My conversation was getting animated too. Sunil's laugh, which I had taken as sinister at first, was nothing of the sort. He was just some drugged up taxi driver out to make a buck, have a bit of a laugh and who could blame him.

I smoked two. Sunil smoked three. Then he took me home. On the way, he asked what I was doing tomorrow. I said I didn't know. It would depend on how much sleep I got. This made him break out in a dirty chuckle.

"Sleep?"

He said he'd take me anywhere in the area next day. I kind of agreed to meet him in the morning at 11- providing I wasn't utterly fucked by then.

When I got in I wrote 30 pages in my journal, smoked another half and felt on top of things.

When it got to 11 I decided to go out, see Sunil and cancel. I was far too wasted for sight-seeing. The elephant training school wasn't happening for me.

* * *

"Hey, Rick- my main man!" he bellowed as I got out the hotel gates. He was propped up on his tuk tuk, shades and a smile dazzling in the morning sun.

"Er. Hello," I said. "How's it going?"

He talked me into going for whiskey at a roadside stall, then I got it in my head to see some temple halfway up a mountain. When it turned out the tuk tuk couldn't go up the incline, I insisted. It seemed the only way to get rid of him.

He dropped me off where the buses went the rest of the way, saying he'd wait. I told him not to bother. That I'd see him in town. He shrugged. "Okay. Well have a nice time."

* * *

The temple had big Buddhas and an expansive view. It also had beggars and tourists in abundance. After twenty minutes I got to leave, down some two hundred steps whose rails were stone dragons.

Halfway down, a woman hawking silk pictures of elephants and shit spread her wares in front of me. I pretended to be interested. It only encouraged her. I agreed to buy one but only on the understanding she'd leave me alone.

"One? Why buy one? Buy two!" she kept saying.

When I finally said "Yes! Alright then yes!" she demanded I buy three.

Broken down by the hard sell, I paid her for three. When I refused to buy more, she turned on me, shouting and screaming "How I buy food for my children? Huh?" She started hitting me with the display case.

I had to get away down the steps, but couldn't move so fast. Everything was slo mo, except this woman like a mosquito, buzzing at me and hitting me repeatedly.

People were pointing and laughing all the way to the bus stop.

Eventually she was restrained by four Buddhist monks who were waiting for the bus.

It wasn't pretty.

IKEA ALIENS

THEY COME IN PIECES.

I grew up in a small Cotswold village called Mickleton, a place so obscure that, to this day, letters sent to residents must include not only a postcode but the line 'Near Chipping Campden' or they will be 'lost in the post'- i.e. chucked in the bin by someone at the sorting office.

Even after the introduction of postcodes, Mickleton still soldiered on with three-digit phone numbers until well into the Eighties. Ours was 285, which was exciting because BBC Radio One also had 285 in its number, but theirs being a London number, it had 6 or 7 digits, enough to make our young minds giddy. And every time they did the Radio One phone number jingle, my sister and I would sing along like it was actually *our* number and we were famous or something.

For an age, the introduction of longer phone numbers was fiercely resisted by the locals. They insisted that the traditional way of dealing with having such a small telephone exchange had worked for previous generations and would go on working so long as folks continued in their time-honoured way. This consisted of an angry local mob driving away any and all newcomers, particularly city folk. However, such outsiders couldn't be held at bay forever. Especially when the angry local mob had had a few pints of cider and couldn't be arsed anymore.

In a masterstroke, my parents subdued the suspicious locals by infiltrating the village as landlord and landlady of the Butchers Arms pub, thereby supplying both cider and a fruit machine to the local rabble. Much as a modern-day meth head might bitch about his dealer but keep coming back for more, begrudgingly our family became an accepted feature of village life.

As a small child, I was fascinated by these cider-drinking sons of toil, mistaking their drunken ramblings for the wisdom of the ages. I remember a conversation I had with them when I was eight in which they all jeered at my claim- repeated from my school teacher- that people were animals too. "We're not bloody animals! We're mammals!" they roared with laughter.

I tried to point out that mammals are animals also. But I got told to go to bed, where I lay sleepless, suddenly aware that even though I was only eight, I was still probably more intelligent than most of the adults I knew.

- – -

Mickleton is chiefly famous for being the northernmost village in Gloucestershire and is located in an awkward taint of county boundaries which means it is a stone's throw from both the Vale of Worcestershire (sprout pickers) and South Warwickshire (ponces). Local landmarks include two pubs, a couple of shops, a church and an old-fashioned phone box that somebody's pissed in.

Looming over everything is Meon Hill, the first outlier of the Cotswold Hills, a ridge that runs south-west to Somerset like an awkwardly displaced spine. Meon Hill was the site of a gruesome murder by pitchfork of a suspected witch in 1945. But as it happened on the other side of the hill, Mickleton's claim to this would appear tenuous at best. Let the Quintons have it. God knows, they need something. They're even less famous than Mickleton.

Mickleton is also infamous (I wanted to say 'famous' but it isn't really and considering what I'm about to speak about, 'infamous' is a much better word) for the Mickleton Hooter, a terrifying supernatural entity described as being, variously, a headless cow, a ghastly hooting sound or a large and spectral but well-formed tittie.

According to F.S. Potter, writing in Folklore – A Quarterly Review (Volume 24, 1914), the Mickleton Hooter is some kind of goblin or Belhowja that *had his haunt in Mickleton Hollow (sometimes called Weeping Hollow), a deep, wooded glen which runs up into the Ilmington Hills, above the village of Mickleton. Accounts of this fearful being having been seen are not wanting, but as a rule he was only to be heard, and that near midnight. His howlings, yellings, and shriekings are reported to have been heard by very many persons ; among others by my maternal grandmother and her sister, who, when returning late in the evening from Hidcote Bartrum to Upper Stoke, had to pass close by the head of the Hollow. The sounds which they heard were enough to alarm them very greatly.*

From my own experiences as a Mickleton child, I can confirm that 'howlings, yellings and shriekings' often woke me around midnight, causing great terror and anguish.

But that was just my parents having a drunken row before bedtime and, while spirits were involved, they tended to be of the vodka variety.

THE MIND-EXPANDING ADVENTURES OF NORRIS SMITH (A BANK MANAGER)
AND HIS JUNIOR MANAGER BARTHOLOMEW JONES
MR. SMITH GOES TO WORK ONE MORNING
OH, NO!. WHERE'S MY BANK GONE?
GONE!
MR. JONES, HIS SECOND IN COMMAND EXPLAINS:
YOU SEE, SIR: THE HILL THE BANK WAS BUILT ON SUDDENLY COLLAPSED!
COLLAPSED? BUT I WAS BANKING ON THAT!
THE END

Black Microdots

My second trip was a black microdot. it looked something like this:

.

I was a naive and impressionable Drama/English student at the time and the size of it led me to conclude it wouldn't do terribly much. So after trying and failing to cut it in half, I ate the whole dot, despite warnings it was off the scale compared to my previous dosage.

I took it with three of my housemates- Paul, who had had a bad trip on Blue Penguins the week before- was the only one who didn't drop.

Within ten minutes, I was unable to get out of my chair. I looked over at the poster on the wall, to find that I could see the shadows around it were a composite of red, green and blue. The curtains started breathing. Then the walls did.

I was aware I needed a drink of water, but couldn't get it myself.

"Paul… Paul," I croaked weakly, "Do you think you could get me a drink?"

Paul tutted and looked at me with bewilderment. I looked over at John who was locked rigid at the other end of the sofa in his own private grinning world. He slowly turned, first into a wolf then into a toad.

"All right now," he said. "All. Right. Now."

"I can't take this. John's turning into a toad," said Ollie. "I'm going upstairs."

I looked back at Paul, the roar of madness ringing in my ears. "Water…"

"Oh, for fuck's sake!" he snapped, going into the kitchen.

I took the glass off him and sipped at it gingerly.

"You can't be that fucked," he said.

"No. No, I can't be that fucked," I agreed, trying to put the glass down on the floor. The pattern of the carpet was playing up my depth of vision, however. I couldn't work out how to get the glass down.

I turned to John. "How long ago did we take this?"

"About. Fifteen. Minutes," he melted.

I wanted my mum.

*   *   *

Five hours later we started to finish peaking. By which I don't mean the trip was over. Far from it. But the initial sensory onslaught, in which I lay on the floor being bombarded by Ollie's happy hardcore tapes whilst tesselating roses and eyes and mouths opened up to eat me., started calming down and something approaching reality began to reinstate itself.

The next thing I was aware of was a knock on the front door. I heard John shouting in his room but the door was closed. I went down the stairs, wondering what was going on.

I opened the door up and there was no-one there. I closed it again, then walked into my room, puzzled. The front door went again. I went to open it again, but once again the street was deserted.

"What the hell are you doing?" Paul had come down to see what the noise was.

“There’s no-one there,” I said, pointing.

“Why are you knocking on the door?” he asked, folding his arms.

“No, there was a knock on the door,” I said.

“No, it was you who was knocking.”

I shook my head, dumbfounded.

“Look, I’ve got a lecture in the morning. Stop knocking the door. And keep it down.” He turned and went upstairs.

* * *

Several hours of psychotic delusions awaited in my bedroom. I couldn’t bear the bare 100 watt bulb and darkness spawned hallucinations. I lay there terrified until dawn came, when the demons on my plaster rose turned into angels.

I later found out that John had spent the night in his room staring at a large knife and wrestling with the overpowering urge to cut into himself and so retrieve his undescended testicle.

Ollie had listened to Sasha tapes in his room.

Daylight gave greater clarity to the hallucinations. I looked out my window at the grey, sleeping terraces which were ultra real under their patchwork of lichen.

Feeling a little better with the sun shining, I decided to go into the kitchen to make a cup of tea. When I went to the kettle it was full of baked beans.

I sat down. Time passed. The phone rang. It was Marny.

“Rick, what the fuck are you doing?” she hissed.

“I’m sitting down right now. I’ve been making tea. But the kettle’s full of beans,” I said.

“And have you forgotten the get-in and technical rehearsal for my bloody play which started an hour ago? Or have you been too busy taking drugs with your housemates?”

Sudden waves of sickness and paranoia crashed over me.

“You make me sick. If you can’t get here then you can forget it. forget it!”

She didn’t say what I could forget, but it didn’t sound good.

“I- I’ll be there as soon as I can,” I stammered, putting the phone down.

* * *

When I arrived at the drama studio (studio is the term in the theatre trade for any poorly-equipped and cramped space that could conceivably be used as a venue), a full-scale row was in progress. I was at least partly to blame, by my lateness, by allowing the time to let lingering resentments reach flash point.

“Get up that fucking ladder!” Marny screamed at me. I grabbed a parcan and started shifting upwards.

Now, it is in the nature of LSD that certain spacial confusions occur. So, looking down from my vantage point in the rigging, the cast looked far away and the ground seemed hard and unavoidable. I span out, nearly losing my footing.

“I think you’ll have to do this without me,” I said, inching my way down.

“And what the fuck is up with you?” Marny asked.

"Well, since you must know I'm tripping my nuts off. I have had a night you people would not believe. I think I'll go home now."

I left.

Looking up into the sky, clouds that looked like Laurel and Hardy rolled into view. Stan Laurel winked at me. It was all going to end happily after all.

Another fifteen hours, and a whole bottle of whiskey later, it finally did.

* * *

Of course, it didn't. The microdot sent us all over the edge leading to three months of mutually-reinforced suspicion, paranoia and loathing. None of us could even be in the same room with each other, let alone communicate. These problems strangely cleared up when I moved out and got a place with some nice girls.

I confess it was reckless and irresponsible of me to do acid the night before something important, but if you can't be reckless and irresponsible when you're young, when can you be?

That's right. When you're older.

The K. Y. Gang

HERE THEY COME!
THE KY GANG
SLURP STICKY SQUELCH SLIDE & SHLOM
SQUELCH
SLIDE
SLURP
STICKY→
SHLOM
GOSH! I'M HAVING SUCH JOLLY WIZZO FUN!
YES, AND LASHINGS OF GINGER BEER!
BUT THEN–
BRRRIING!
CRUMBS! THAT'S OUR CALL!
INTO ACTION, KY GANG!
SO–
WHERE WAS THE CALL, SLURP?
IN THE PARK, BEHIND THE BANDSTAND!

IN THE PARK~
SORRY GEORGE
OW! THAT HURT! YOU TOLD ME IT WAS A SAFE LUBRICANT! BOVRIL INDEED!
NEVER FEAR! K-Y ARE HERE!
GO, GO, GADGET LUBRICANT!
WOW! WHAT LUBRICATED JOY!
SPLATTA!

THANKYOU, WHOEVER YOU ARE!
WE'RE THE KY GANG - WE'VE SAID IT TWICE THIS SKETCH ALREADY!
K.Y.
BACK AT KY HQ-
QUICK, GANG! MRS. MIGGINS HAS GOT TIDDLES STUCK AGAIN!
INTO ACTION!
HOME
AND-
OH, THANKYOU, K.Y GANG!
BLESS MY HOUSE
THINK NOTHING OF IT, MRS. MIGGINS!
MEOW!!

OH, OKAY! PISS OFF, THEN!
EEK!
MROWL!
QUICK! I'LL FORCE IT OFF WITH A JET OF HIGH PRESSURE K.Y. JELLY!
COR!
SLOOSH
HOORAY! WE'RE SAVED!
ALL FOR ONE & ONE FOR ALL!
K.Y.
KY
KY
KY
KY
CENSORED

THERE'S PLENTY MORE FISH IN THE 'C'

Growing up in the sticks in the 1970s meant for much of the time we had to make our own entertainment. A favourite game played in the family was Hide and Seek, in which I would invariably hide under my bed.

Although this would seem an obvious place to check, I very rarely got found. I thought this was because I was just brilliant at Hiding. Only years later was I told that this was actually because nobody was Seeking. They had merely suggested the 'game' as a ruse to get rid of me and my incessant "But why?" questioning.

Typical conversations between my junior self and my mother went along the lines of:

ME: Why is the sea blue?

MUM: Because the sky's blue.

ME: But why is the sky blue?

MUM: Because it just is.

ME: But why?

MUM: Because I said so, that's why.

ME: But why?

At this point, I'd often get a smack- to which my reaction would be to go hide under my bed and sob quietly. If her patience wasn't entirely frazzled from working a 16-hour day in the pub, she would suggest a game of Hide and Seek and I'd go hide under my bed and try not to breathe too loudly. This could go on for hours.

Under my bed seemed like it could hold all sorts of adventures and I firmly believed that some kind of helter skelter portal to another land might be revealed one day, just like in Jamie and His Magic Torch. I would switch my electric torch on and off repeatedly, hoping that this time the magic hole would appear to take me away from Mickleton.

Only it never did.

Once in a blue moon, we would be taken to the Regal Cinema in Evesham, which had a curved screen that genuinely acted as a portal to rich and strange worlds. I wasn't sure which was more magical- the images on the screen or the blue wisps of cigarette smoke rising up from half the audience that flickered and danced in the light of the projector.

- - -

The first time I ever went to the Regal Cinema was to see the 1976 remake of Dino De Laurentiiissississ's King Kong, starring Jeff Bridges and a gigantic animatronic gorilla, when I was just three years old.

I must have been very affected by the film because, right at the end- when King Kong climbs to the top of the World Trade Center in New York, and he's grabbing at helicopters and gets shot and falls to the ground; and he's bleeding and obviously dying- his enormous gorilla heart slowly winding down- I leapt out of my seat near the back of the gods and ran as fast as I could to the front, tears and snot streaming down my hot, chubby little face, and screaming over and over again "Don't die King Kong!

"Don't DIE, King King!

"DON'T die, KING KONG!

"DON'T DIE, King KONG!"

The fact that the audience all started laughing at me somehow made my grief worse. Was a world in which King Kong could not only die, but be laughed at in his final moments really somewhere I wanted to grow up?

I vowed there and then that when I got home, I would go straight to under my bed and never come out ever again.

Looking back on it, I realise that I ruined the end of the film for the entire cinema audience. But as it scores a measly 5.8 out of 10 on IMDB and 46% on rottentomatoes, they probably didn't mind much either way.

As for King Kong, I'd like to think that he got his revenge and that stomping around on the roof of the Twin Towers caused some sort of structural weakness, which would result in the buildings falling into their own footprint at free-fall velocity on September 11th, 2001 after being hit by a couple of planes.

It's about as plausible a theory as any for what actually happened that day.

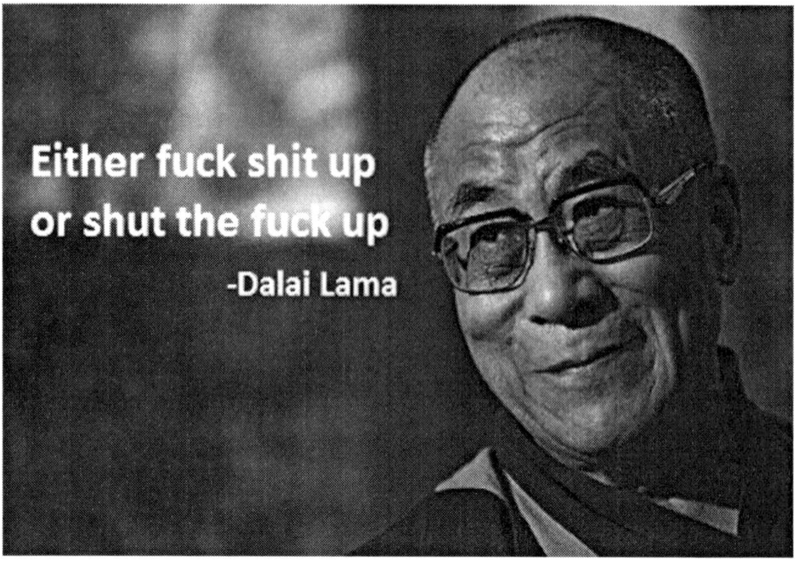
Either fuck shit up
or shut the fuck up
-Dalai Lama

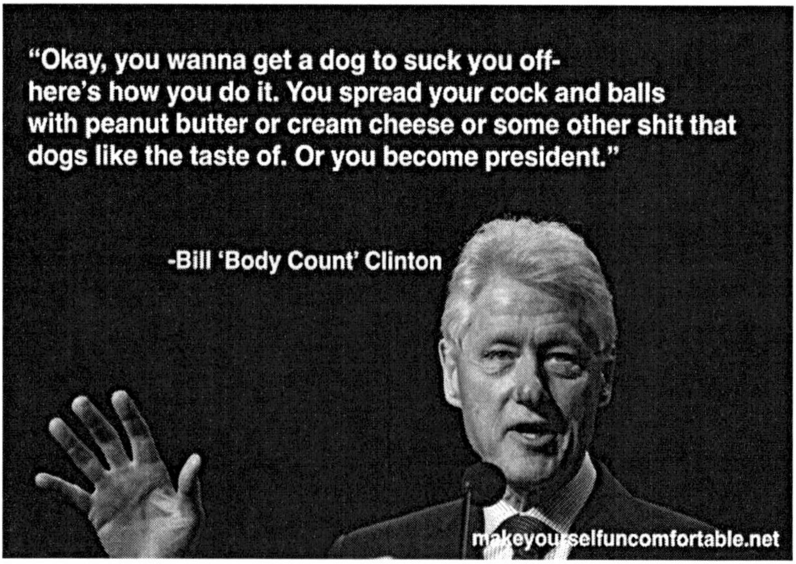
"Okay, you wanna get a dog to suck you off-
here's how you do it. You spread your cock and balls
with peanut butter or cream cheese or some other shit that
dogs like the taste of. Or you become president."
-Bill 'Body Count' Clinton
makeyourselfuncomfortable.net

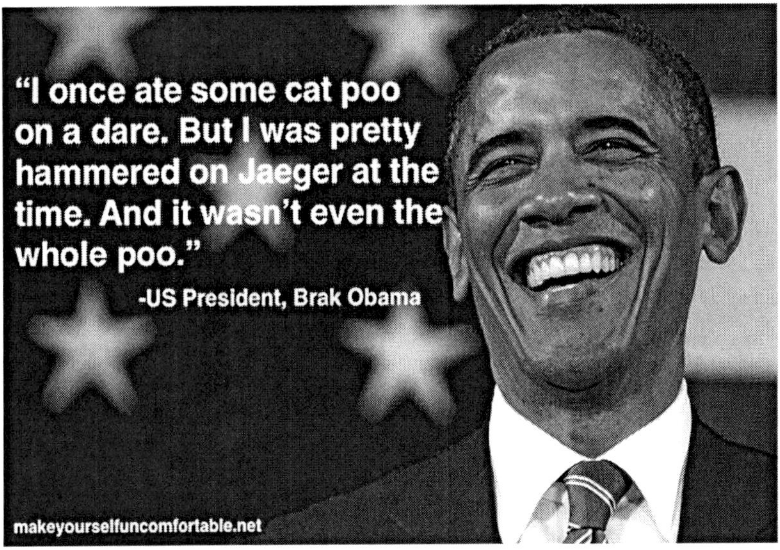
"I once ate some cat poo on a dare. But I was pretty hammered on Jaeger at the time. And it wasn't even the whole poo."
-US President, Brak Obama
makeyourselfuncomfortable.net

Despite being Queen one has always suffered from sour and lingering farts. Having corgis gives both constant companionship plus something to blame the eggy odour on.
-Her Majesty, Queen Elizabeth II
makeyourselfuncomfortable.net

My Terrist Confession

I like terra firma

And couldn't be without it

Except on a boat

And even then I doubt it

So maybe I'm a terrist

-I fit the description:

I say up yours! to unjust laws

And keep sharp knives in the kitchen.

I live by a semi-detached 'e' state

In a terrist house

In a terrist street.

I love love, basically, and hate hate

And am cutting down on meat.

I'm cutting down on shopping, too
-All these things that I don't need
Don't please me like they used to do.
I'd rather smoke some weed.

And I'd rather keep the fruits
Of all I labour at each day
Than have some rich old reptile
Lock it all away.

I'd rather folks took action
And questioned what they're told
Than bow to dodgy factions.
Man, it's getting old.

I'd rather we dropped tools than bombs,
Then went outside to play

Or at least went out

For a beer, anyway.

Anyway, I'm a terrist.

My ideas are a poison.

IGNORANCE IS STRENGTH
FREEDOM IS SLAVERY
WAR IS PEACE

Well, enjoy son.

First Rule of Bottling Up: Don't cut your fingers on the broken glass in the sludge at the skip bottom.

Second Rule of Bottling Up: Always rotate the stock. Remove existing bottles, wipe shelf with warm cloth and place new stock at back, making sure to wipe and face each up.

Third Rule of Bottling Up: Be finished by 11am when the customers start arriving. Nobody wants to see a ten year old busy behind the bar.

- – -

It was such rules as these, not explicitly written as above, but learnt at my father's knee and the pointing of his pipe, that shaped the weekend mornings of my childhood years.

Life in a medieval Cotswolds pub at the start of the eighties was a harsh existence, made worse by unheated bedrooms and an excessively Victorian dad- who wouldn't even let us watch Grange Hill- but on we struggled, dragging coal and lighting fires, polishing bottles and chopping wood, my sister and I.

For three pounds a week, and a copy of 2000AD thrown in for good will, I laboured each weekend to ensure the smooth running of the pub. Obviously I shouldered the burden with some grumbling, having friends whose parents gave them twice that just for playing Atic Atac all day, but my folks considered that working for my keep would instil both an awareness of the value of money and a sense of duty in me at an early age. I remain to this day a reckless spendthrift. Such is life.

I was better off than some of my friends however, who if they wanted money at all would have to go round all the bins in the village retrieving empty Cresta bottles for the 5p each was worth. When times were hard it was worth doing, but it seemed to all of us that the bottles that came with a deposit were getting scarcer. The skip I had to empty out at the pub twice a week had seen progressively less of its bottles sorted out and packed into crates ready to be returned to the brewery. More and more, I was just chucking them in the bin.

It was a particularly deposit-less month for my friends who were hanging out ready for me to finish my chores so we could go off to the rec. They were kicking the ball to each other on the car park when a juddering wagon, some relic from the fifties, pulled up onto the front. We knew the truck, just as we knew the driver who waved at us from its cab, gurning and turning his false teeth round for our child-like amusement.

It was Bob Mooney, local dealer of scrap metal and anything dodgy that needed shifting. In earlier days, he would have been classified as a Rag & Bone Man- in fact some of the village elders did call him this- but by Bob's own admission he was a Scrap Metal Dealer. I suppose nowadays he would be down as a Reclamations Consultant or some such bollocks, but he's almost certainly dead now so we've no way of checking. And in the unlikely event that he still actually is alive, he was totally illiterate when I knew him and firmly held the view that "Reading is for poofs."

Bob Mooney also had a sideline, something that wasn't profit making, but appealed to the Irish tinker sheer bloody love of watching a fight that was in him. For many years he had acted as a boxing mentor/coach for dispossessed local lads, giving them the old Rocky Balboa routine before psyching them up to beat seven bells of shit out of some other kid at some village hall or other.

He had made quite a name of himself, too- his gurning grin, false teeth poking out crazily, had adorned many of the sports pages of the local newspaper (it was that, pig wrestling or cheese rolling). he had developed quite a reputation for training up winners, as well as towing cars away. Now he had a problem, which was why he was pulled up on our drive.

“Alan, I won’t beat around the bush,” Bob Mooney began, his face black with soot in his grimy, besmirched boiler-suit, as he stood before my Dad in the pub bar. “I know you’re a busy man. And I also know that your skittle alley is empty on a Sunday morning, am I right?”

“Ye-es,” the Old Man said, not giving much away. “What of it?”

“You see it’s like this, Al- I’ve got a real winner on my hands, this lad I’ve got boxing- a real cracker, but we need somewhere to train. Now, I’m not a rich man, but I can afford something- you know.”

My father was mentally calculating.

“And, what we’ll do is maybe open it up as a club for boys in the village who want to come and spar, train up. It’ll make real fighters of them.”

My father said he’d get back to him.

After that, he asked me if I wanted to box. He assured me it was sporting.

I asked if I could get out of bottling up on Sundays if I did boxing practice. He said he’d have to think about it.

Eventually, he came back to me with an offer. If I did boxing club I didn’t have to do the bottling up on Sundays in the main bar. I’d still have to do the skittle alley, plus skip out in the main bar. My sister, who would pick up my relinquished duties, was insistent.

My friends, who were hyped up by now on account of watching Rocky on VHS, were nagging me, asking when they would get the chance to be boxing tough guys, plus it might be a cool way to impress girls (as far as any of us cared about that sort of thing). I thought about it some more before agreeing.

Junior Fight Club was on.

* * *

I quickly found out that it was at least as boring as bottling up and about fifteen times more effort. Junior Fight Club, far from being a bit of heroic battling to the strains of Eye of the Tiger, was actually a load of skipping, running on the spot and going "Hoosh! Hoosh!" whilst punching the air. All this was while Bob Mooney concentrated on his protege, the wild gypsy boy from Broad Marston.

"That's it, Champ! Kill the bastard!" screamed Bob Mooney, trails of saliva being ejected from all round his dentures, whilst the wild gypsy boy hit the punch bags with psychopathic hatred in his piggy little eyes, all the while going "Hoosh! Hoosh! HOOSH!"

Bob Mooney would turn from a bout of this, when the Champ went off to skip up a fucking rope for all I cared, and menacingly utter "Now. Which one of you boys wants to spar next with him?"

We would all shake our heads, point at each other, feign sprained wrists; anything to avoid having to spar against the Champ at Bob Mooney's Junior Fight Club.

For a start, the Champ was about four years older than we were, and when you're a ten year old squaring up to a fourteen year old you don't stand much chance. Particularly if the fourteen year old in question is a trained and vicious thug on his one-shot chance of avoiding prison. All of which meant he won a lot of bouts and was now within a hair's breadth of his first belt. He just needed training, which was where we came in: to act as punch bags and give the Champ a moving target to aim at.

"Hoosh! Hoosh!" he would say in the sparring ring, testing out a couple of jabs as he weaved his way towards you. "Hoosh! Hoosh! HOOSH!"

On the third "Hoosh!" he generally hit you as hard as he could, unless you managed to duck in time. If he hit you it hurt. He concussed all of us at one time or another. Him and Bob Mooney always seemed happy more than concerned at these moments.

In terms of the members of Fight Club, apart from the Champ, I think Bob Mooney thought us a sorry bunch. I much preferred Frogger or Pacman to any sort of physical activity in any case and my friends were similarly underwhelmed by the concentration and dedication that goes with being a boxer.

None of us were thick enough.

We all began to find Fight Club a bad idea, but it was me who got out first. Like so many other activities I tried out, I at last hung up my gloves after a particularly violent battering.

And after I had hung them up, I took a surprise swing at The Champ, knocking him off his seat and drawing blood from his nose.

And yet it was *me* who got bollocked for being aggressive.

STARDATE 2358 AND THE SPACE STATION 'WEIRDICUS' HAS AN EMERGENCY -
MAYDAY! MAYDAY!
SO -
LISTER, I'VE JUST RECEIVED A MAYDAY CALL FROM THE WEIRDICUS.
YOU MEAN -SIR?....
...EXACTLY.
IT SEEMS THEY'VE BEEN DOING THEIR OWN ACCOUNTS.
CRIKEY!
YES, AND WHAT MAKES IT WORSE IS THAT THEIR STOCKS ARE DOWN. SOMEONE IS EMBEZZLING, BUT THEY DON'T KNOW WHO.
A TERRIBLE BLOW, SIR?!

NO THANKS, LISTER—MY WIFE GAVE ME ONE THIS MORNING. WE WANT YOU TO RENDEZVOUS WITH STATION AND SORT OUT THEIR ACCOUNTANCY PROBLEMS!
THUS, NIGEL LISTER BLASTS OFF IN THE ROCKET 'NIRVANAMIND'
AND ARRIVES AT THE 'WEIRDICUS'
THE NAME'S LISTER. NIGEL LISTER - INTERGALACTIC CHARTERED ACCOUNTANT!
I SUPPOSE YOU'VE COME TO READ THE BLOODY BOOKS, THEN.

AND SO-
HMM! THIS IS WHERE THE PROBLEM IS! SOMEONE FORGOT TO CARRY THE TWO OVER WHEN ITEMISING THE CHEESE ROLLS—AND THAT 'SOMEONE' IS...
CAPTAIN CAT!
YES—IT WAS I, LISTER! AND NOW YOU DIE!
NOT SO FAST, KRAUT!
WHAM!
NOW TO GET OUT OF HERE QUICK!
EXIT

LISTER ESCAPES THE 'WEIRDICUS' IN THE 'NIRVANAMIND' MERELY SECONDS BEFORE...
...THE WHOLE SPACE STATION EXPLODES!
BOOM
LATER
...SO YOU SEE, SIR, AFTER FINDING THE BOOKS WERE WRONG I PLANTED A NUCLEAR CHARGE & BLEW THE WHOLE STATION TO KINGDOM COME!
WELL-WELL DONE, LISTER. LET ME BUY YOU A PINT!
CHEERS, SIR!

It may be a little hard to believe, but I actually started out my career (as in 'careering out of control') as a children's entertainer.

It was all down to that bloody drama degree, of course. Once I had got a taste for the smell of the crowd and roar of the greasepaint, what was there to stop me? Well- reality, maybe, but that's another story.

I applied for a few acting jobs from The Stage and eventually got taken on by the West Midlands Children's Theatre Company for a four-month tour round the country performing a piece called 'Harlequin's Holiday' to appreciative audiences of three to ten year olds (if you were eleven, the whole thing kind of sucked).

Inspired by Commedia Dell'Arte, only without the arte, or the commedia (unless flying sausages make you chuckle), the play had a cast of three- two men and one woman who, in a commendable nod to equal opportunities, played the Harlequin. She also played the love interest, which was handy because it meant the company could pay less wages. There were five or six other groups also performing the play at the same time.

The first week of touring made me realise that the song 'Hi-Diddle-Dee-Dee' wasn't giving the full story of what an actor's life is about. Far from lying in bed till after two, we were up every morning at five before driving for three hours to that morning's show. We might have two morning performances then another drive before an afternoon show at another town, probably miles away from the town we were at first thing.

After getting the set up, we would have about twenty minutes to prepare ourselves in, which generally meant drinking coffee in the school staffroom, having slightly strained conversations with the teachers, before it was time to rush off and get into our tights.

And I don't mention tights metaphorically either- I had to wear thick, black woollen tights that were guaranteed to make the older boys piss themselves laughing when I flounced on stage in a purple tunic and ruff. I still shudder, thinking about those costumes. They were all kept in a suitcase and laundered whenever we had a chance- which, given we were doing twelve or fifteen shows a week, wasn't often. God, they stank.

During that first week, the tour manager/other male actor and the girl playing Harlequin got drunk and ended up shagging. The tour manager thought he was on to a good thing here so, when it was time for us to relocate up North, he took the liberty of booking a double room for them and a twin room for me which I had to myself. For one night only.

Harlequin was horrified and gave him the 'you know, we need to have a professional relationship here' speech, followed by the 'I've just decided I'm not that sort of girl' routine, which meant no more nooky.

The tour manager, who was on a cocktail of mindbending prescription drugs for his various personality defects, took this rather badly and tried to get me to side with him to have her sacked. She was trying to get me to side with her also, so I had to put up with them both bitching to me about each other for the next few weeks. I didn't really take sides, as I thought they were both twats, but my sympathies were definitely with her. God knows why she slept with him though- you do the casting couch before getting the job, not after.

Every evening, the tour manager would get horrendously drunk until two in the morning, drug himself up with chill pills, then wake up three hours later and insist on driving. He refused to let me or Halequin drive, not wishing to give up that little bit of power and control (as he saw it) that driving the van brought. This despite the fact we were taken on specifically because we had driving licences.

As I said before, the play was specifically aimed at little kids, yet the owners of the company would take any booking. One day we found ourselves arriving at a young offender's institution where surly youths jeered us from the windows as we pulled up. When one shouted we were "All fucking dead!" as we were dragging the set out of the van, I flinched, hitting my head on the door frame, which concussed me and drew a fair bit of blood.

Even had I not been concussed, it would still have been a horrific performance, what with the constant interruptions from inmates in the courtyard banging on the metal screens over the windows and gesturing that either particular audience members were dead or, on more than one or two ocassions, us actors. It was hard to concentrate, what with still bleeding and the menacing sniggers and remarks of "Fucking wankers" and "This is fucking shit" coming from the audience. We decided to cut out two whole scenes so the play didn't make any sense at all, and got out of there as fast as we could.

After a few weeks in the North, the tour manager decided we would spend the rest of the tour based in Coseley, the home of the Company, just because he liked the pub round the corner from the digs.

Coseley is an awful dump in the Black Country. Our digs, above the company offices, were indescribably bad. Three different groups of actors were staying there at any one time, so I had to share a box room with four other guys. One snored and another one stank.

There was no heating to speak of, save for a gas fire that hadn't been safety tested in a decade. It belched out carbon monoxide, giving us all headaches. The landlord, the brother of the woman running the company, advised us to leave a window open if we were going to turn the fire on- which, to me, defeated the whole object.

I got a mate to post me an eighth of soap bar each week, which I would smoke in the kitchen, wondering if this was really what an actor's life was like. For a great number of them it probably is, barring the long periods of unemployment euphemistically referred to as 'resting'.

I began to understand how military people feel towards the end of a gruelling tour of duty.

As we limped towards Christmas, I convinced the tour manager that, for his own well-being, perhaps going on the road again after only a three week holiday wasn't the best idea. Not if he wanted to retain whatever scraps of sanity he had left. Strangely, he listened to me, and decided to give himself a break. Last I checked, he was in his friend's unfinished film project- a zero budget comedy about aliens or something in need of crowdsourcing.

I also opted out, wanting to spend a while at home to recover, although the directors of the company told me that I could tour with them again any time I wanted. It's an offer I've yet to take up.

As for the West Midlands Children's Theatre Company, I later found out that the reason our contracts were non-Equity was that we were working at least fifteeen hours longer each week than was legal, plus were getting paid about half of what we should have been. It also didn't help that the guy who ran the company had punched the lights out of one of Equity's directors at a charity dinner some twenty years before.

CHEMIST SHOP JOKE
SCRIPTI
TRY DURACELL CONDOMS-LAST
EXCUSE ME—HAVE YOU GOT ANYTHING FOR SPOTS?
CERTAINLY SIR—HERE, HAVE 48 MARS BARS!
MARS
YOINKS!

When I was nine, growing up in The Butchers Arms, Mickleton, a religious sect from California moved into the large property over the road. This was a rather grand building, whose privet hedges kept my sister's stick insects in food.

It was called The White House, due mainly to it being painted white, not through any resemblance to certain other white houses, except it too was inhabited by American nutters.

The White House, Mickleton nutters were at least taking their cue from the more positive aspects of spirituality- peace and all that, rather than some Old Testament vengeful git of George Bush or whatever Barak Obama is supposed to represent. They were Californian head cases rather than rabid Christians and/or closet Islamic Jihad, after all. I gather there's a difference, although I'm astonishingly ignorant about such things. I went to California once and it resembled some car park by the sea through which astonishingly large people wandered, shopping.

Checking out their website, it says that

The mission of Emissaries of Divine Light is the spiritual regeneration of humanity. We believe this to be the most pivotal factor in the world today.

This may sound fair enough now, but at the time it was mightily disturbing to the villagers, supping pints of cider in the bar.

So, they were in touch with their spirituality, but did this give them any right to go about looking so insufferably smug? To an isolated, rural community (there was no bus service- my parents had two cars which I wasn't allowed to drive, being only nine; I had a bicycle, but it was a Grifter, so even going to the shops on it was an effort) it was like the Invasion of the Body Snatchers.

To combat their undeniable sinister takeover, they went on a charm offensive, inviting all the kids in the village to attend their prayer meetings. This annoyed the vicar of St. Lawrence's no end, who up until then had had the monopoly on indoctrinating the youth with fairly sinister nonsense.

When they started buying up several large properties in the village, including the mansion house, the national media came knocking.

Well, ringing. I guess.

In any case, Newsnight on BBC2 carried a special report, all of it done to the theme tune from The Archers, and delivered in a strong West Country accent (which was wrong anyway because this was The Cotswolds and a bit less burry- a technicality, maybe, but geography is geography), giving the nation the tale of superstitious, rural folk menaced by a strange new force that they didn't understand and didn't much care for. Much of it was filmed in the pub.

Outside the pub, my dad was interviewed as a prominent local businessman. He loved that. He wore his blue blazer with gold buttons and frothed at the mouth about these outsiders coming here and invading the local community, which was a bit rich really because he was from Birmingham.

It cut to the Emissaries. Who were they? What the bloody hell did they want?

"Well, we believe in peace," (or something), droned a guy with a beard (I'm dredging this from memory: I taped over the VHS with Raiders of the Lost Ark a few years later, in protest at my parents' divorce). He held up a fuzzy felt picture he swore was Charlie Brown, shown in a wheelchair with his leg in a cast.

"Why are you so resentful, Charlie Brown?" Beardie Weirdie asked, in the kind of voice reserved for kids and dogs, leaning in to take in the answer should one be forthcoming.

“See,” he carried on, as the picture didn’t respond, “He’s got this broken leg of resentment, but he needs to lose that. He needs to heal and move on. Yes, sirree. Charlie Brown needs to get out of that chair and smile.”

At this he nodded to the interviewer in a sagely manner, which was undermined slightly by Charlie Brown’s fuzzy felt leg falling off.

Life for a while was an uneasy coexistence. Me and some of the other kids would cycle up and down in the lane outside The White House, just should anything funny kick off, but because I had a Grifter I got tired out after about ten lengths.

The only eventful development was NBC News turning up from America to do an item on the cult. They pitched up a camera on the pub car park and filmed a couple of hours of us kids riding up and down. So maybe I got on American TV, struggling with the hefty weight of my Grifter, maybe not. The NBC archive doesn’t seem terribly accessible to members of the general public.

More Emissaries moved into the village. The place became like a Stepford movie thing, all happy Californians in jump suits bobbing up and down the lane with the blissed-out smiles of those who had entrusted their whole essence, including bank details, to some Supreme Being or other.

Just as it seemed the village was about to be destroyed by the Emissaries’ disturbing grinning, the sect scaled back operations. I think the IRS possibly clamped down back at their spiritual home on Sunshine Ranch following allegations against the leadership of sexual misconduct, drug taking and all the standard things one would expect to get up to running a cult. I could well be mistaken in this, however, should any members end up reading this and fancy suing me (I don’t have anything to sue anyway, so good luck with that).

They had to sell up practically everything, except Mickleton House which they now hire out for conference facilities to help pay for the loony brainwashing.

The Manor House got turned into luxury flats when it was sold off, so, in the end, the village got destroyed by a much worse force than the Emissaries.

Yuppies.

Jamie Oliver, French for 'I like Oliver', is a billionaire television chef with a chain of successful restaurants, a hot wife and a much-discussed disgust for Chicken McNuggets.

He is also my nemesis, because I could so easily have been Jamie Oliver. The parallels are there.

The fact that I am not is all my parents' fault, of course.

We both grew up in family-run pubs and both had to help out from the age of eight. Jamie's parents put him to work in the pub kitchen, where he spent his time chopping and peeling vegetables, slowly learning how to prepare and cook food. He would go on from this to become a world famous celebrity with oodles of cash.

My parents, by contrast, had me chopping wood for the fire, stocking the bar up, and changing beer barrels, slowly learning to enjoy the taste of stale beer. And, after my early career as a pyromaniac fizzled out, I would go on to become a bitter, penniless alcoholic.

In 2001, I finally caught up with my nemesis as he walked, hand in hand with his wife Joolz, past the Pig and Fiddle pub in Bath. I was outside on their beer patio, having a drink with my sister.

Both of us decided that Jamie and Joolz would find it hilarious and touching if we started shouting "Joolz! Joolz! Jamie! Jamie!" until they turned around.

Thrillingly, they did.

Jamie cocked an eyebrow, questioningly.

"It's pukka, mate!" I managed to bellow. "Fucking pukka!"

I held up my glass as if to toast them, but rather than smile in grateful recognition at this fanboy display, Jamie simply shook his head, whilst mouthing something that looked very much like “Wanker”, before walking away forever.

But I think the best gig I *ever* got was when I used to entertain a fair few people (the rest would just get irritated) as the mascot for Stratford Upon Avon's local radio station The Bear102FM (I would love to be able to direct you to a live feed, but they closed down years ago).

This meant, unsuprisingly, dressing up as a large bear (a dancing version of which is the heraldic symbol of Warwickshire) and doing my bit for the 'troops' (shoppers, really, but it's all part of the war effort, keeping up morale) by standing waving when the mayor cut the ribbon to a new discount shoe warehouse or burger chain.

Sometimes, when the mayor wasn't available, for jumble sales and the like, which his office would consider 'non newsworthy' (even the Stratford Herald has its limits), I got to cut the ribbon myself. This was something I always dreaded- those big bear gloves are a nightmare for handling scissors with, but I think I dealt with it with quiet dignity (it was a non-speaking role).

I opened Shoe City and some Londis-type store in Bidford-on-Avon, and no matter how cynical and jaded we may become, that's still got to be a good moment for anyone.

Most of the time though, the bookings got me down. There was never anything useful for me to do. Once we had gone beyond the initial clamour, swift disappointment set in from the crowd because

a) the bear didn't talk

b) he didn't do much else either

It wasn't *my* fault. As any insider will tell you, nine times out of ten a bad performance is down to a bad director. Either they give you too much direction, saying I want this this and this no you go stand over there look just do it because I said so that's why, or they just leave it wide open. In this case, I felt there was a notable lack in this department.

Beyond getting the suit drycleaned, the station really didn't give me much assistance. I tried listening to their programmes, thinking maybe I could get inside the character of the station and thus the bear that way. But the music bored me to tears, so I switched it off.

* * *

At gigs, people would remark that the bear didn't look very happy as I shuffled glumly in a corner. What they failed to understand was that, in my own characterisation of the bear, I realised that pathos played a huge element in his existence. Being cruelly forced to parade around shopping estates for the benefit of a local radio station trying to gain kudos from its attachment to a new Jacksons Mini Market would be enough to upset anyone. And particularly a bear.

Ok, you're a **bear**. I thought, trying to get into the part. What do you *really* want?

Honey sprang to mind. Trampling over picnics sprang to mind. Lady bears sprang to mind. Avoiding hunters sprang to mind (this is an example of the kind of processes one goes through mentally when establishing one's role. Budding thesps take note!)

How unnatural an environment for a bear, then, patting children on the head at the end of an aisle of fish fingers.

In character, my big, bear heart was broken.

How could I wave?

* * *

One late afternoon, following a whole day of not smoking tobacco, in which I vowed I would be free of the evil curse of Nick O'Teen, I got the call for a gig at the Studley Car Boot Fair Annual Guy Fawkes Fireworks Night (Parking £1.50). One of the other bears had dropped out and they needed someone reliable and they needed someone fast.

It would be my first bear roadshow. In fact, I think it was the radio station's first roadshow too. It was a biggie, but I answered their call. The call of the wild.

* * *

But when I was actually at the gig, my mind wandered feverishly. Like some smackless junkie, I was withdrawing from the nicotine, and it hurt.

Lots.

I felt my whole bear mask slip.

Not my actual bear mask, of course, which was securely attached, but my inner bear 'mask' (if you like), through which I articulated the gargantuan primordial savagery and sadness of the bear, as well as the commercial interests of the radio station. If some mums and dads were happy too then, well fine.

Behind the trailer, the DJs were all smoking cigarettes and talking about the kinds of (inane) things radio DJs talk about. I looked over at them, desperately craving a hit of nicotine before I went on stage.

I was so wrapped up in needing tobacco, that it clamoured out any thinking in my brain. I wasn't aware that, on stage, they were announcing me.

"It's the bear!" cried the DJ on the stage, three maybe four times.

Eventually, people started tutting.

I got it back together.

"Where do you think he could be?" I heard the DJ announce over the PA.

Consummate professional, I thought, focussing. Obviously knows a thing or two about improv.

"Let's give him a count down. 5 – 4 -3 etc."

This time, I made it. I climbed up and onto the trailer without falling over.

It was the worst performance of my life.

I had been thrown, you see. And once a serious actor. I mean a really really serious actor. Loses. That- that, **connection** to the *essence* (I suppose), then the whole thing falls flat.

It didn't matter that I was in a full body bear suit. I was naked up there.

Terribly, terribly naked.

And lost.

And alone.

And naked.

Even though I didn't have my cock out.

* * *

When it came to handing out the prize for the best Guy Fawkes, I gave it to the wrong kid. Apart from that, and although they were all chanting that they wanted the bear to show them his little dance, I just stood there, blinking out at a sea of people from Redditch who were getting fed up because the fireworks hadn't started.

When I came off I immediately smoked three cigarettes, lighting each one off the butt of the last.

\- - -

And now, children, it's ***your*** *turn to get creative with a wonderful colouring-in picture of some bears on the next page. Take out your very best felt tips and get scribbling!*

I am completely off my tits right now

"That's not God – it's just a dog going backwards."

I'm not much of a religious man
-you wouldn't catch me praying
to the body of the bleating lamb
or cattle a-laying.

No
something tells me God
is a disgraceful old sod
and Heaven's a club
for all-night raving,
& me and you
must line up and queue
while He's in there and on it,
glow sticks waving.

Soon we'll see His lights,
pick up the P.A. playing.
The Word is that it's Good tonight,
so we don't begrudge paying
though we're not sure still
who's on the bill
and nobody's saying..

And nobody leaves:
They keep letting more in.

Out here it's hard to say
If that's a good or a bad thing.

* * *

Michael
the bouncer
bursts into view,
chucks out the chavs
checks out the shoes.
A quick once-over
And we're through.

Next is the turn
of the totty on the till
who tots up your treachery
in an itemised bill-
each drunken lechery
each ill will;
and if you have problems
with the means to pay
she'll refer you to a social scheme
with a place to stay
in Purgatory. Paradise is still yours,
of course,
you'll just have to come back the long way.

As I approach
she pulls out my list-

quickly scans one night stands
and millstones to grist,
promises broken
nonsenses spoken,
chances I'd missed;
a catalogue of catastrophes, in short,
that when I see it in writing
makes me pissed.
But when she totals the bill
It's less than I thought;
maybe they just keep records
of cases that reach court.
Still, it's informative to find
that most of my evil was just in my mind .

* * *

I get through the gates,
Sidle up to the bar:
"Serve me a Stella
or, failing that, ambrosia."

Now, I don't mean the creamed rice
Made by cows in Devon
And frankly I'd be surprised and disappointed
to find semolina in heaven.
No there's no mushy peas
blues reds greens
no crack clam chowder;
no b's no e's
mind your q's and p's
lose your wrap of powder.

These are poisonous supplementaries
that do not cure or heal or ease
the pointless carryings-on in town
of the cash and carry crap heads
that got you down.

They are all gone now,
All's soft and warm.
Jesus has needled us.
It's a shot in the arm.

And yea, if it should happen
That we gurn or we gouch
Jesus will lead us
To the safety of a couch
And He won't call our parents
Or shine a torch in our eyes
Or point out our pupils
Are quite the wrong size.

He won't say he gives up
or that really it's beyond Him how we thought we'd ever get anywhere in this world by the telling of lies,
anywhere in this world
by the getting of high.

Anywhere is somewhere.
We get by.

Well, I've rather rambled again;
I've friends to see
At half past three
On an ethereal plane.
Must get a move on
to avoid the rain.

You must stop by sometime again.
Visitors welcome.

Heaven's boring.

Every night's the same.

B.L. Sibbub
Tee Hee
He's a little devil!
ONE DAY-
BEGONE, THOU GOD FEARING MORTAL!
SHUT UP AND GET DRESSED, BRIAN, OR YOU'LL BE LATE FOR SCHOOL!
I AM THE SON OF SATAN! SEE! I HAVE THE SIGN!
DON'T BE SILLY BRIAN, THAT'S JUST FELT TIP!
BAH! HUMBUG!

AT SCHOOL-
RIGHT-GET OUT YOUR BOOKS, CLASS!
HA HA! TAKE THAT, YOU WORTHLESS SON OF ADAM! CACKLE!
GUFFAW!
BRIAN! HAVE A HUNDRED LINES AND GIVE ME THAT FORK, NOW!
NO FEAR! I'M OFF TO JOIN MY TRUE SATANIC FATHER!
IN THE LOCAL SHOP
HELLO, SONNY-WHAT WOULD YOU LIKE?
SOME FIRE-LIGHTERS,

HOW OLD ARE YOU, SONNY?
I'M THE ANTICHRIST! I AM AGELESS!
THAT'LL BE 20p PLEASE
I'LL NOT PAY YOU
:CRACKLE!:
IN PARK-
NOW TO GO AND SEE DAD!
LOOK! BRIAN'S BURNING HIMSELF ALIVE!
:CRACKLE:
:WOOOF!:
HURRAH! TIME FOR A FEAST!

Sick as a Dog

Stratford-upon-Avon, 1996.

Following University, I went to live at my mother's. This was in recognition of the twenty quid she had sent each week, which kept body and soul together, during my last term. My father had been no use at all, having got his second wife to send me an emergency parcel containing three Vesta curries, and that was purely through spite.

My mother's house, following the squalid speed-enhanced freedom I had grown used to, was pretty staid. They watched TV most evenings before turning in early. I, meanwhile, would be awake half the night, hanging out the window smoking soap bar joints and feeling miserably trapped as I surveyed the roof of Safeway's beyond the garden fence.

The soap bar I would get from my mate Dave who lived up the road. He dealt dope and played his decks as loudly as he could in the house he had appropriated through an ingenious petrol coupon scam.

It wasn't that ingenious, really. Dave had got lucky and found two large boxes full of these blank coupons they gave you each time you filled up your tank at Shell.

Now, normally petrol coupons got you fairly rubbish stuff- glass tumblers maybe or a chart CD. Not so this offer, aimed at commercial users and offering no end of good stuff you could have if only you had the coupons.

Dave estimated that he had found more coupons than the average taxi firm could expect to get in a five-year period. The only snag was that they needed stamping with an official Shell stamp.

Corruption and low pay being what it is, it didn't take Dave long to convince the night cashier at the local Shell garage to go in on the deal with him. Being the night cashier he also didn't think to question the 10/90 split, which was a bonus from Dave's point of view.

They stamped and stamped for days- morning, noon and night. With the proceeds, and following some story or other to Shell, Dave got enough stuff together to sell on to afford the deposit on his house, whose living room he turned into a shrine to comfort, loud music and drugs.

His girlfriend wasn't too happy with this, but he could never hear her above the noise of the techno so it didn't matter. He had heard it all before, in any case- her umpteenth complaint about the disreputable stragglers who would stop by to score. It didn't make any difference to him.

Soap bar, as dealt by Dave to a good many school-aged citizens, is the most noxious form of marijuana there is. In fact, it is difficult to classify it as marijuana as it quite often contains no THC at all. Instead, the makers of soap bar throw any old brown shit together that they can find, whack a load of tranquilisers in and bind the whole lot together with glue. As a rule of thumb, the harder the solid is, and the more difficult it is to burn, the more binder has been used in manufacturing, and the worse its quality is.

We didn't care. I dare say we didn't know. At the time I was happy to chug it down by the bucketful.

Red Seal at fifteen quid a quarter sounded a good deal, until I later learnt just how cheap the stuff is in bulk. Much later, I would find out Dave had been under-weighing me also- giving me 6g instead of 7g but who was I going to turn to? Weights And Measures?

* * *

While I lived with my mum and stepfather, they decided to get a boxer dog that they called Bruno. Probably after Frank. He was their pride and joy.

As a puppy, he was absolutely uncontrollable, being huge and excitable, and desperate to get anywhere you were, even if it meant jumping all over you. He was cute yet annoying.

My mother and stepfather doted on him, but also made sure to properly train him. Every time he pissed, my mum would stand by him, repeatedly saying “Wee! Wee! Wee!” Eventually he got so he pissed whenever she said this.

One evening, I came back from work to find both my folks in a state of distress. My mother was sobbing hysterically. Even my stepfather had tears in his eyes.

“What- what’s wrong?” I asked, steadying myself for a shock.

“It’s Bruno,” my mum sobbed. “He- he collapsed.”

“Collapsed?” I dumbly repeated.

“We’ve taken him to the vet’s and he said” – here she choked back tears with a heaving sob- “He said, ‘I’m afraid that your little doggie is going to die!’”

* * *

When her crying had subsided, mum explained to me that Bruno had been his normal bouncy self that morning, then round about midday, he had suddenly collapsed. She couldn’t get him to respond. He just lay there in the garden, eyes rolled back and his tongue lolling out, in a vegetative state.

Mum was alone with him at the time, and, panicking, had called up my step dad. He came home from work right away, and together they had taken the dog to the vet.

The vet had been perplexed. He had only seen one similar case in a boxer- a botched tail docking which had led to damage of the central nervous system. The dog had had to be destroyed. Of course, he didn't want to jump to conclusions, so had taken a stomach sample and was keeping the dog under observation. It didn't look good, however.

"It's no fooking use!" my stepfather said, slamming his fist into the door. "Our poor bloody dog's going to go and fooking die!"

"And to think how much we loved him. And cared for him, and" – my mother began, before heaving into sobs again.

"That's too bad," I said. "I hope he'll be okay."

To get out of the way, I decided to take myself off to Dave's where we listened to ear-splitting gabba and took turns to do gravity bongs with two litre bottles.

When I got home, it was late. I opened the front door quietly, taking time to turn the key, and crept near soundlessly to my room.

I closed the door and leant across to my stereo, pulled out a tape and put on my headphones.

It was a bummer about the dog and no two ways about it, I thought, pulling out my tobacco pouch and lighter and going to the drawer where I habitually kept my stash.

It wasn't there.

I closed the drawer, blinked a few times and then opened it again. Sometimes this did the trick. Admittedly not often, but in the state I was in it was my best shot.

The ruse proved a complete failure.

Where my stash had gone remained a mystery that evening. Soon after I had faced up to the fact that it wasn't there, I crashed out, only waking when my alarm brought me back to shrill awareness, the tape still on auto-repeat in my ears.

* * *

At work that day, in between feeling shafted and humiliated in general by capitalism, I pieced it all together.

I was in the canteen towards the end of my lunch hour, idly wondering if a little smoke might enliven the afternoon, when I remembered that my gear had gone missing. Mentally, I tried to place it. I had last had it soon after I had scored it from Dave, leaving it in the pocket of my shirt rather than in my drawer. The shirt had been left on the floor. The dog had obviously found his way into the room and eaten the gear. Occam's Razor (or whatever) in this case was the greedy jaws of a puppy who ate anything interesting he came across.

All that afternoon, I had a strong and sincere hope that the vet hadn't looked for marijuana during his analysis.

* * *

My mother, when I got home, was still worried. The dog had come round a little, she explained, but was staggering round at the vets and was so unstable and just plain poorly that they had given him a big shot of steroids, in the hope it might revive him. The stomach analysis had turned up nothing. All they could do now was wait and hope.

I kept quiet.

The next day, when the effects of the soap bar wore off, and with the massive dose of steroids really kicking in, the dog sprang into sudden life at the vet's, scaring the shit out of the veterinary assistant who had given him up for dead. She was so surprised, she let him get past her to go running and jumping around barking in the car park and out into the street. It took some time, apparently, to get him back under control.

They called him Lazarus down the vet's after that. Which shows an impressive grasp of biblical stuff.

* * *

One drunk Christmas about six years later, I finally confessed to my mum and step-dad. By then, they found it funny. But they were rather drunk at the time and I think the next morning they had forgotten all about my confession.

I have yet to remind them.

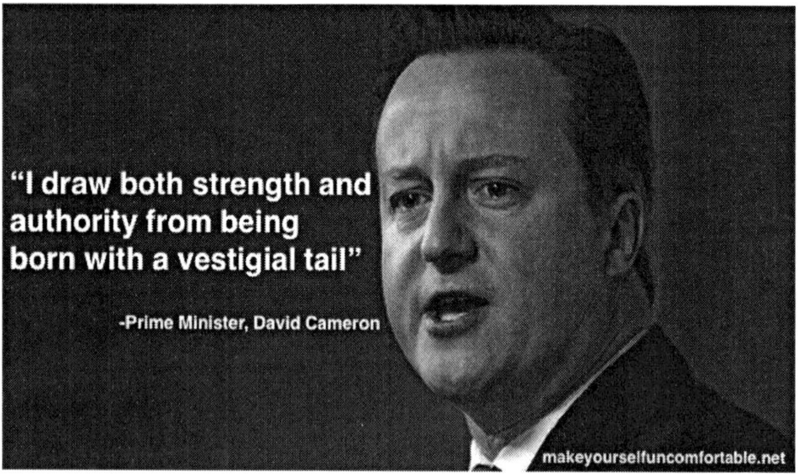
"I draw both strength and authority from being born with a vestigial tail"
-Prime Minister, David Cameron
makeyourselfuncomfortable.net

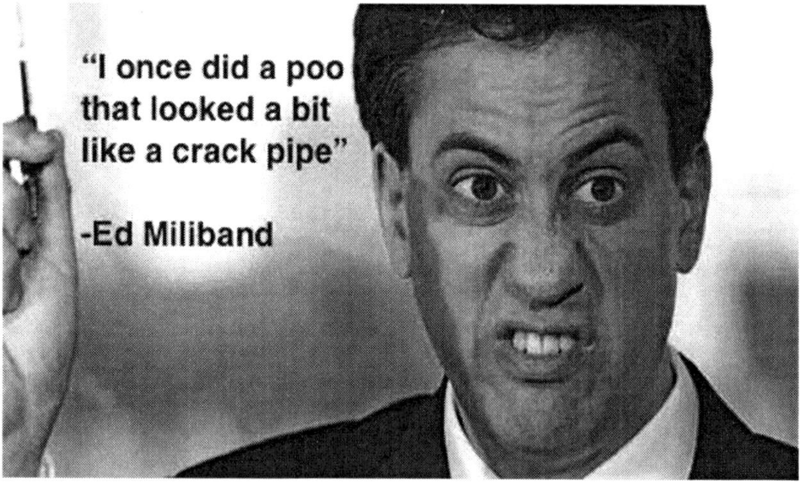
"I once did a poo that looked a bit like a crack pipe"
-Ed Miliband

Possessed by possessions
lord & master of all we owe,
belonging to belongings:
it's a disaster, I know.

Chained to the mundane,
our reference frame
is physical;
every day
the same old same,
nothing metaphysical.

And if God's not dead
he must be mad
or blind
or deaf & dumb
or bad,

still smarting over Christ,
perhaps,
the way the people
have been had.

But in our defence
I'd like to say
we nearly chose
the proper path
but lost the plot
along the way.

You've got to laugh.

It’s not our fault,
it’s just the toys
we made
made such a lovely noise

and girls
and boys
are high and dry.

Time to bid
all this
goodbye.

LT.
ATENSHUN!
BRANSTON PICKLE
BY RIK
4.A.M.–
Z
WAKEY WAKEY, RISE AND SHINE!
UH?
GET UP, YOU 'ORRIBLE LOT!

GEORGE, DEAR-WHAT ON EARTH ARE YOU DOING? IT'S FOUR O'CLOCK IN THE MORNING!
SILENCE! I WANT THE WHOLE COMPANY ASSEMBLED IN THE DRILL HALL IN FIVE MINUTES!
BUT THAT'S THE KITCHEN!
AND SO-
RIGHT! LET'S HAVE A ROLLCALL! NAME AND NUMBER FROM THE LEFT!
DON'T BE SILLY, GEORGE-YOU KNOW PERFECTLY WELL WHO WE ARE!
DECEMB
RIGHT, SOLDIER! ANY MORE INSUBORDINATIONS AND YOU'LL BE FACING A COURT MARTIAL!

THIS IS BLOODY RIDICULOUS! I'M GOING BACK TO BED!
HOLD IT RIGHT THERE!
DESERTION IS IT, EH, SOLDIER? NOT READY TO DIE FOR YOUR COUNTRY?
FOR GOD'S SAKE! HE'S ONLY TWELVE!
YOU'RE IN ON IT TOO, EH? WELL, TAKE THIS, TRAITOR!
BLAM!
EEK!
JESUS CHRIST! YOU'VE JUST KILLED MY MUM!
HEH! WELL, SOME CASUALTIES ARE UNAVOIDABLE!
PTUI!

JESUS! I'M PHONING THE POLICE! YOU'RE BLOODY BARMY!
HALT!
DECEM
KER BLAM!
NOW TO NOTIFY THE PROPER AUTHORITIES...
AND THAT'S HOW IT HAPPENED, SIR.
WELL, PICKLE...
THEY WERE OBVIOUSLY COMMUNIST SPIES. HERE-HAVE A MEDAL!
YOINKS!

Stratford-Upon-Avon, 1997-1998

Once upon a time in a land far, far away (Warwickshire) I used to work as a theatre technician. I don't mean a medical theatre- all clamps and tubing and bits being hacked off- but a theatre for the Performing of Arts.

It wasn't a real theatre, actually, although I later managed to blag some work at the Royal Shakespeare Company off the back of it. No, this was student theatre, or more accurately the School of Performing Arts (and Music Technology, tacked on as an after-thought) at Stratford-upon-Avon College.

Now if 'School of Performing Arts' conjures up images in your mind of big-haired show-offs in leg warmers bringing New York traffic to a standstill with star jumps and choreographed routines whilst singing their little hearts out (bless), then you're getting old.

You're barking up the wrong tree also. This wasn't NYC it was SOA, and the students weren't Italia Cunti-type stage school moppets. No, they were BTEC (British Training Something Something) students from Brum and older folks studying for their HND (Have No Degree) at the largest Further Education Drama Department in the country.

Here, three hundred delicate egos, each the size of Cumbria, would be put through their paces and challenged by working on some of the greatest contemporary theatre going (and all really good art has to be challenging). It was an experience that undoubtedly stood them in good stead for a future of stopping people in the street on behalf of various charities.

* * *

I had blagged my way into the job, knowing absolutely nothing about the technical side of theatre whatsoever. I didn't even know a Phillips from a flat-head. But this being arts education, nobody seemed to mind. None of the other teaching staff really knew what they were talking about either- they were just winging it and hoping for the best too, so I fitted right in.

My job title was Technical Assistant. Below me there was a General Assistant who had been taken on at the same time. He knew even less than I did, having dropped out of education altogether to study death metal and motorbikes, so got £500 less a year. Above us both, however was The Technician.

The Technician was a grotesque, fat freak of a woman with features like an undercooked ready meal. You are what you eat. She was meant to train us up, an idea nebulously floated in by the newly-appointed Head of Department, a company yes man who been given the job, not because he was the best candidate, but because he had agreed to do whatever the College Management wanted. The other teachers didn't like him much, and would speak contemptuously about him when he was out of earshot.

"Have you had yer training on the rig, yet?" he would ask.

"No, and I can't find The Technician," I would say. "I think she's out on another errand."

I later found out that her 'errands' consisted mainly of gassing with the ladies in Finance and going into town for long lunches.

Students would rush up to me in her absence with some crisis or other.

"What do we do? What do we do?" they would panickingly demand, eyes bulging out with primadonna stress.

"I dunno," I'd shrug. "I haven't had any training, have I?"

Six weeks into the job, The Technician went on long-term sick leave with 'a bad back'. When it turned out she was moonlighting elsewhere and wouldn't be returning, we weren't surprised. Although the General Assistant and myself were a bit concerned.

* * *

I quickly learnt to rely on the Technical Theatre students. From my first contact with them, when I had handed out the wrong screwdriver, they and I knew the situation. The Techies were to cover my sorry ass in return for being allowed to hang around the Resources area, which they thought gave them kudos. Perhaps it did. They were incredibly enthusiastic and knowledgeable about the whole techie thing. I, however, was professional (in that I was getting paid to be there).

At the time I was doing a lot of clubbing and would constantly play techno at frightening volumes, frequently rendering nearby lessons unworkable. I didn't care. I just sat there, wiring up lights and sipping tea, acting all surprised if I got asked to turn it down.

"So, what do you plan to do after college?" I would ask students during impromptu counselling sessions in Resources.

"Well, I really want to act," they would reply, all starry-eyed, thinking about the limelight.

"Well, tough- you can't. I've seen you on stage and you're rubbish," I'd say, if I felt they needed to wake up and smell the coffee (or if I was on comedown). "Have you thought about a job in I.T.?"

* * *

I might not have known much about technical theatre during my sojourn at the School of Performing Arts, but one thing I certainly did know about was taking drugs.

So when I got challenged one Sunday evening by a bunch of students I had bumped into in The Water Rat (don't go looking for it, it isn't there any more) to drop acid with them, I only had to consider it for a few minutes.

"Go on, drop one with us," they urged.

"I dunno, folks," I said. "I've got work in the morning."

"Yeah, well we've got college too," they said. "So what? Don't you think you can handle it?"

This was like a red rag to a bull.

"I can handle double what you can," I said, wagging my finger at these floppy-haired teens calling my reputation into question. "And don't you forget it!"

"Well, prove it then!" they jeered.

Five seconds later I was swallowing a tab.

I won't bore you with the details of the trip. They all came back to my flat, some of them got freaked out, some of them didn't. I was aware that Monday morning was rapidly approaching, and then remembered something that had slipped my mind in the bar- that my week-long First Aid At Work course was starting at 9. Oh shit.

That was when I got freaked out.

* * *

10am saw me hallucinating wildly in the middle of a conference room floor, attempting to perform CPR on a dummy whilst a room-full of unimpressed council workers looked on. It was one of the hardest experiences of my life. The lecturer had to help me up in the end after I just lay there, holding onto the doll instead of giving it the kiss of life. I couldn't get my head round what I was supposed to be doing, much less co-ordinate my body.

Eventually lunch time arrived, and with it the worse case of flu I have ever had, which came on suddenly while I was trying to eat a sandwich. I was just getting to the crusts when I collapsed.

I stood up and managed to shakily make my way out and off campus. When I got to the main road I was holding onto things to keep myself on my feet. By the bottom of the road, I was crawling on my hands and knees, sweat pouring off me in buckets.

I was in bed for a week after that, feeling the illest I have ever been.

If there's moral in all this, I don't want to hear it.

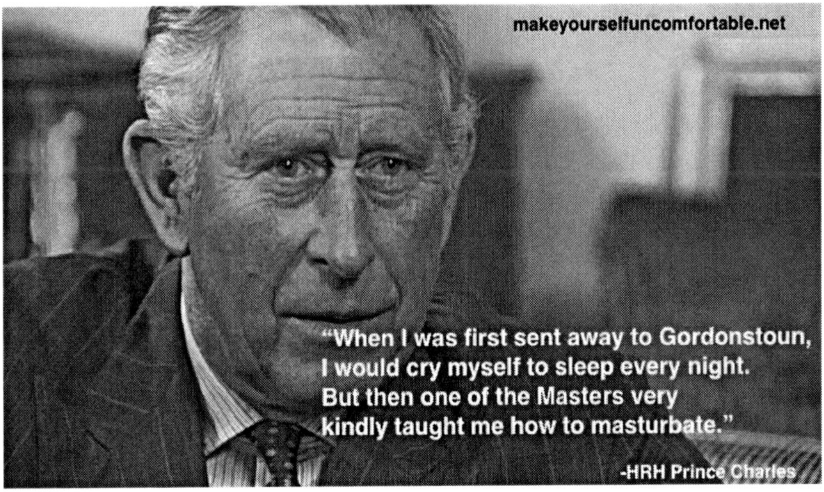

The first time I got arrested was in Birmingham in 1996.

I had gone out clubbing with a mate of mine, both of us big techno heads and pretty much addicted, at the time, to Atomic Jam and House of God.

But we decided we needed a change. Techno nights played fantastic music, but they were always short on women. Either women didn't like the music (a sweeping generalisation- I knew quite a few girls who dug it) or they weren't impressed by a bunch of sweaty druggies in hooded tops. I dunno.

So we thought we would go to Wobble, a house club famous for its bouncy wooden floor. When everyone was dancing, the whole place wobbled.

About ten minutes after the pills started kicking in, we both realised that the club was utter shit. Fatuous househeads drifted by, coked up to hell and sneering at each other. The music could have come from Woolworth's.

We looked at each other and, as one, decided to leave. Just going home to chill out and listen to decent music would be better than this.

My mate had parked his car just outside the club, so we left and tried to make a quick getaway. We had only gone a couple of streets when a flashing blue light in the rearview, combined with a whooping siren, let us know we were about to have a tet-a-tet with the boys in blue.

Minutes later, we were sat in the back of a police car, our hands cuffed behind us, under arrest for £5 worth of marijuana they had found in my mate's car. The strange thing is that my mate had had a pill on him, in a plastic cash bag, which the police had given back to him, then left us alone, probably to give him the opportunity to swallow it.

As they drove us to the station, one of the police turned around, saying "You know, it's amazing. We've pulled everyone leaving Wobble tonight and every single one of you has had drugs on you. I think that says something about that place."

"No, I think it's says something about youth culture nowadays, officer," I replied.

Back at the station, the pills I had taken were really starting to kick in. I knew I was in trouble, but the whole situation seemed unreal. I've said it before, and I'll say it again- fluorescent jackets are real; flashing blue lights are real; the police are a social fiction. So how could I recognise them as any sort of authority?

When you get busted, they ask you for all your details- weight, height, hair colour, aliases- that kind of thing. When the officer asked me my eye colour, I said "Hazel".

"Hazel?" he asked, sneering. "Well, they're black fucking holes right now. You've been on something, haven't you?"

"Yes, officer," I replied, sighing. "I've taken two ecstasy tablets."

He leapt up then, overjoyed at the ease of my confession. "Right," he barked, pointing at me and turning to the other police. "I want this man strip-searched."

I was led into another room, where I had to remove one item of clothing at a time. And this is the thing- the male officer who had ordered the strip search was quite clearly letching at me. He also looked disturbingly clone-like with a big Freddie Mercury moustache. Probably being in uniform was a bit of a fetish for him. I stood naked, with a cock like an acorn, feeling miserable, yet strangely defiant.

Next I was fingerprinted, mug shot taken, and banged up in a cell for four hours. In the cell, the pills- some of the strongest I had ever taken- made me feel like I had one motherfucker of a case of flu.

Eventually, they let us go. We had been promised a lift back to my mate's car, but the officer who had made this empty promise had gone out again to bust more heads.

"We were promised a lift," my mate was saying to an underwhelmed desk sargeant. "We don't know where the car is."

"Well that's what happens when you take drugs, ennit?" he laughed. "You can't remember where things are, can you?"

"It's not about remembering. We're not from Birmingham. We don't know where you arrested us."

It was to no avail. We were left to wander the dirty streets of Digbeth until the car was spotted.

So, my first arrest and experience of how dumb police really are, criminalising and bullying people who would normally be decent, law-abiding citizens. I got a three year caution for possession of one gramme of soap bar, and one fuck of a chip on my shoulder about 'the law'.

Remember, it's not a War on Drugs. It's an attack on personal liberty.

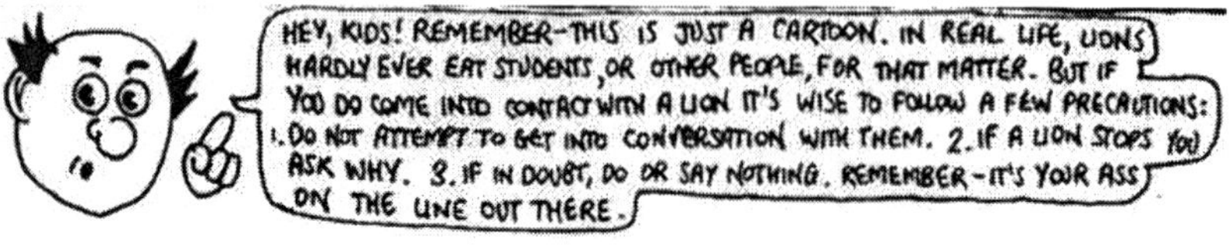
HEY, KIDS! REMEMBER—THIS IS JUST A CARTOON. IN REAL LIFE, LIONS HARDLY EVER EAT STUDENTS, OR OTHER PEOPLE, FOR THAT MATTER. BUT IF YOU DO COME INTO CONTACT WITH A LION IT'S WISE TO FOLLOW A FEW PRECAUTIONS: 1. DO NOT ATTEMPT TO GET INTO CONVERSATION WITH THEM. 2. IF A LION STOPS YOU ASK WHY. 3. IF IN DOUBT, DO OR SAY NOTHING. REMEMBER—IT'S YOUR ASS ON THE LINE OUT THERE.

so i got asked what cultural stuff i been doing in thailand… think i went past a temple the other day… or it may have been the Novotel…other than that, it's been shrugging off the ping pong show touts mainly who act like there actually may be a ping pong show going on somewhere… it's that one where ping pong balls get fired from a lady's doodah rather than just watching a game of table tennis. Because as a form of drunken transgressional entertainment, watching people playing ping pong just doesn't cut the mustard…

and for days I kept saying no, no, no, no thank you. finally I said "oh, huh, ok then" to some tout, lured in by the offer of a free show all evening so long as I buy a minimum of 1 drink … so I go in and there's an empty stage with all these bored looking girls with numbers on, and all suddenly springs into life with the arrival of their first customer … so I order a Beer Chang and they tell me it's 2000 Baht (about 40 quid!) so I laugh & say no way … they say "hey hey! no problem! floor show start now.. ok!"

a semi-obese woman in her mid to late fifties hobbles asthmatically up onto the stage, hitches up her skirts, grunts and then shits out a dazed-looking goldfish, which plops into its waiting bowl in a clearly traumatized state… entertainment for the dangerously psychotic, perhaps, but not the ping pong show as advertised. the one with the ping pong balls.. anyway.. so i go to leave… one or two of them say "why you go now? is coca cola show next" … i thought- shit- if it's the same coca cola routine they were touting 12 years ago- and if its the same woman as the goldfish routine then i simply do not wish to see her humiliating herself on a cheap conjuring trick, just for an audience of one-

FUCKING ME, WIV ME FORTY QUID CAN OF LAGER

the coca cola bottle trick is hardly up to the standard of a david blaine illusion, I grant you, excepting the fact they're both performed by cunts.

it's one of those tricks that's kinda novel due to the unexpected use of a common or garden object- in this case, the lady bits, juxtaposed with something that you wouldn't normally expect to appear coming out of a doodah (e.g flags of the world, a caricature of amy winehouse, the last remaining shreds of dignity); in this case, it's a jet of what looks exactly like coca cola being squirted into an empty coke bottle with not one drip dropped…maybe; the coca cola bottle trick is a bit like a soda stream, except a fair bit ruder (taste-wise they're probably about evens) …

so i figure i gotta get the fuck out cos it's crap.. and the original tout tries to grab me, saying I owe for beer … he (or it might be she, tbh) says I opened the beer and now I gotta pay and yadda yadda yadda. the beer wasn't opened (nor had it been chilled either) I run like the wind, children, if the wind had had about 5 pints and a couple of tequilas… and for about 400 metres i have this tout still grabbing onto my T-shirt until I manage to get away…

the moral of the story is – avoid "Money Night" in Patong. …

in fact, why not save the money you would have wasted in a hole like Money Night by simply buying some ping pong balls (or stealing some) so you can have your very own "ping pong show a go-go" in the comfort of your own home. or somewhere else.

YOU WILL NEED:

(1) a set of ping pong balls;
(2) a vagina (or easy access to one);
(3) the ability to queef on demand and in a controlled and safe manner (this is so you don't accidently pop someone's eyeball with a dart when you've graduated to balloon bursting);
(4) Practice! Practice! Practice!

… and when you're ready, invite friends*, family*- everybody* in to witness the poetry of ping pong a go-go

*OVER 18s ONLY. NO FLASH PHOTOGRAPHY

DINCO PRESENTS THE CARTOON ADAPTATION OF
St. DiNSMarg
LOOK AT THIS SUBTLE GRACE PEOPLE OFTEN ASK ME WHERE I COME FROM AND I USUALLY SAY MY MOTHER'S VAGINA.
NO, BUT SERIOUSLY, UNCLE VULVA! I COME FROM HENLEY IN ARDEN - A SMALL ISLAND NEAR THE SOUTH POLE
ANYWAY, I'D LIKE TO SHOW YOU ALL A MAGIC TRICK - PICK A CARD.... ANY CARD!
IS IT... IS IT...
IS IT THE THREE OF CLUBS?
COR! AMAZING!
READER'S VOICE

Stratford-Upon-Avon, 1997.

The months after my father's death were strange, dark ones.

Ripped off for every penny in the will and thrown out of the family home by my Wicked Stepmother, I was forced to take, at immense expense, a shoddy ground floor studio flat on the Alcester Road in Stratford-Upon-Avon.

Its electricity supply was via a pound coin meter, which was ever hungry for whatever I could feed it, which wasn't much. Eventually, I lost half my wardrobe to an aggressive mould and most of my mind to a growing sense of desperation at the state of my life.

Some two or three years before I moved in, the place had been run as a brothel, called, rather wittily, the 'As You Like It'. All that was in the place's past, though. I used the room mainly for necking ecstasy, something I ended up doing every single night of the week, alternating it with amphetamines, until my poor, fragile brain reached the point of near collapse.

As bright light started to upset me, I replaced the bulb in the room with a red one, giving it a seedy atmosphere that suited well the dark mood I was descending into.

When I was 'entertaining' a couple of friends one night, a guy turned up at my door at about 3am, asking if he could 'come in for a cup of tea'.

Something in his desperate and hurried tale of pursuit by the police in Coventry made me suspect that perhaps 'cup of tea' was some sort of code.

I told him I only had instant coffee, but it was only after I had closed the door on him that I twigged he was after a shag with a prostitute.

I changed the red light to a blue one after that, but that just made me paranoid about the police. So I then went with an orange one, like out of a fake electric coal fire.

On one particular occasion, I had been staying awake on base amphetamines for the three days leading up to the weekend, just because it seemed like the thing to do. A few of my friends came round that evening to drop pills.

We had scored 'X-Men', thick, speckly pills with Xs on, hence the name. Everyone was sensible and took only one. Everyone, that is, except myself and another guy, who shall remain nameless.

Actually, he won't, otherwise the story will be that much harder to write.

Let's say his name was 'Fred'.

Fred. Yeah, that'll do.

As the drug took effect, Fred and I looked at each other, a strange half-panic in which we realised we had, to put it mildly, overdone it.

"Shall we er, go for a walk or something?" Fred asked.

"Definitely. Need to go and err, get a drink, I reckon," I replied, half blinded by the rush.

We staggered out into a changed landscape, colours blooming randomly in the dark, and set out on the path behind my house that led, eventually, to a Shell garage.

As we walked, we passed Stratford-Upon-Avon College, where I was then working.

“Shall we go sit down for a bit?” Fred asked. “I feel a bit sick to be honest.”

This seemed like a good idea. Nausea and a sense of foreboding were gripping me also. We walked over to a bench and slumped down on it.

We tried to talk, but consciousness kept coming in and out like the tide of the sea. Only much faster. It was as if we could see the auras of trees, bushes, all that was living. The sky seemed alive, clouds rolling and boiling across a full moon that lit up everything in its glow.

“Look at the clouds, man,” I said. “They sure look weird tonight.”

“Look at that bit of the sky,” Fred said, pointing.

Where he pointed, a section of the sky seemed to light up, then formed into a definite rectangular shape.

“That’s pretty odd,” I said, taking it in.

“Sure is.”

As we both watched, the rectangle lit up more definitely, then, like the curtains of a theatre, the clouds rolled back to reveal the sky behind. Only it wasn’t just a night sky. Pulling the curtains back were cherubim and seraphim, definite entities that were eager for the show to get underway.

They revealed a procession of ancients sitting on thrones, so many going past that our minds boggled.

“Wow, do you see that?” I asked.

“Yes, I do,” said Fred. “Old men on thrones.”

Things sped up. The thrones gave way to a succession of images. We saw a rat being eaten by a cat, being eaten by a dog, being eaten by a lion, and so it went on. The animals then became dinosaurs, all of them.

"What do you mean?" I asked the sky.

Again: the animals of the world appeared, all tessellated like pieces of a jigsaw so that, together, they formed a perfect whole. One by one, the pieces turned dark until all that was left was darkness then this too was replaced, once again, by dinosaurs.

"You mean we're going to become extinct?" I asked. We both knew the answer. A huge face appeared in the sky and nodded.

"But why?" asked Fred.

The face melted away and we could see factories, smoke and pollution, cars and tanks, then massive explosions, Hitler, armies marching, misery and suffering. It was terrible to behold.

"But what can we do?" I asked.

The face reappeared, this time we could see its body as well. It shrugged, as if to say "sorry- nothing."

I groped for something to say. "Well, peace man," I managed, giving the figure a peace sign. It smiled, and returned the sign, before turning and walking back into the clouds.

"Wow, oh wow," Fred was saying, "I do not believe this."

"Nor me, but- I think that was God," I said.

Right on cue, the clouds parted again, this time forming a stairway, up which countless angels ascended, surrounded by the whole host of heaven.

"I think that maybe we should go back," I said. "Tell the others."

"Right."

We sped back to the flat.

Some techno was throbbing out of the stereo. My mate Dave was smoking a joint and chatting to the other people in the room.

"Wait!" I cried. "You've got to come outside- there's mad shit going on in the sky."

"That's right," said Fred. "Angels. God. It's incredible."

"Come outside", I urged, "It's miraculous!"

Dave pulled on his joint and narrowed his eyes. "Just what the fuck are you two on about? Shapes in the clouds? Don't be ridiculous. We've all seen those."

"No, I mean it," I said. "I've never seen anything like this before. It's amazing. I think God's been talking to us."

"You're making a complete fool of yourself," Dave said. "Both of you- how many drugs have you two done?"

"I'll come out," said Louis. "I've always wanted to see God."

"Fine," said Fred. "Let's go."

"I'm not going anywhere," said Dave. "The whole lot of you are being nuts. I'm rolling another spliff."

"Fine," I said. "You do that."

We left, going back outside, Fred excitedly telling Louis what we had seen as we walked up the path to where we could get a clearer view of the sky.

"There!" said Fred, triumphantly, showing Louis. "What do you see?"

"Erm, well-" said Louis. "It's just clouds really, ennit?"

Fred and I looked at each other, incredulous. We could still see angels and dinosaurs. Suddenly a pterodactyl swooped overhead.

“Fuck me, a pterodactyl!” shouted Fred. “Did you see that?”

“Yeah, I saw it,” I said. “Big wasn’t it?”

Louis looked at both of us for a moment, before saying, “Well, I can’t see anything. Maybe I should have double-dropped too, eh? I’m going back inside.”

With that, he turned and walked back to my flat.

“Well, what do we do now?” I asked.

“I’m getting a camera,” said Fred. “I need to capture this! Let’s go to Dillons, get one of those disposables.”

“Well, okay..” I said, but I already had a sinking feeling that maybe this was just a hallucination. Or maybe you really needed to be extremely off it to see this order of reality. I wasn’t sure which.

It was getting light by the time the two of us reached the newsagent.

“I need a camera,” announced Fred. “I’m about to take a photo of God!”

The assistant was taken slightly aback, but then regained his cool. “Sure, whatever. Have fun lads,” he said, handing over the camera with a nasty smile.

In the car park on the way back, Fred took picture after picture of the clouds, saying stuff like “Wow! Snakes! You see them snakes?” and so on.

I could see them, but at the same time I could also see them as clouds, as the pill was beginning to wear off.

After a while I said, "Look, I'm going back to the flat. Are you coming?"

"Not yet!" shouted Fred. "I'm waiting for God to come back!"

Needless to say, he didn't.

When I got back to the flat, Dave was sat there, still smoking a spliff.

"You made real fools of yourselves there, you know that," he said.

"Really?" I asked, crushed.

"Damn right. Seeing things in the sky? Ever heard of hallucinations, maybe?"

I sat down, dejected. Fred then burst in, chattering away about what he had seen until everyone shouted at him to shut up, and that if he couldn't take his drugs and behave then maybe he shouldn't take them at all.

Finally, I was forced, by peer pressure, to admit that I hadn't really seen anything, that it was just my over-active imagination. I even asked Fred to be quiet, not because I didn't believe him- we had shared the experience, after all- but exposed to the inquisition of my friends' ridicule, I would rather keep it private.

I haven't really heard of a shared hallucination before, but apparently ecstasy can cause some sort of telepathy due to the way it excites certain brain receptors.

As a postscript, Fred went a bit funny after that, some sort of mild breakdown. I'm sure he's fine again now, though.

God knows.

I haven't seen him in years.

LE CLUB
SORRY, SIR – IT'S MEMBERS ONLY TONIGHT!

Following the 'seeing-God-in-the-sky' episode, I realised that, in my attempt to upload myself to a higher state of consciousness through huge quantities of uppers, I had broken through my ceiling and everything was crashing.

Those friends of mine who had been foolish enough to join in on a year-long binge of untold chemical madness, were starting to "bug out" also.

Alex, who had been taking multiple drops of liquid LSD on a daily basis, flipped out during a cinema visit to watch The Exorcist. He was sectioned under the Mental Health Act for running down the street naked, screaming at people to come out of their houses; the aliens were about to land and Alex wanted everyone on board the mothership.

For my own part, I stopped taking ecstasy, amphetamines, LSD- everything really, in an attempt to rebalance my mind.

It didn't work.

Weeks slipped by in which I felt I was drowning, unsure who I was any more and barely able to function. How I managed to keep my job at the College I have no idea.

I wanted medical advice, but I didn't want to get sectioned myself. So I took a trip to the doctor, told him the death of my dad was making me so anxious anything might happen. I was careful to avoid talk of suicidal tendencies, but told him that I had tried Valium before and had found it very useful.

The doctor was initially taken aback. Used to prescribing old folks with haemorrhoid cream, he didn't know what to do or how to proceed. I took the initiative.

"You see, I've been self-medicating with all sorts of things for years," I said.

"Well, now, I really don't want to be encouraging the misuse of drugs."

"But I won't be misusing them. I'm in pain, doctor. Psychological pain. I get these anxious episodes, when I'm alone at night. I just need something while I'm in these early stages of grief."

"Normally we recommend counselling," he began, tapping his pen on the pad.

"If you won't prescribe me then fine," I said, "You know, there's plenty of other substances out there on the streets to mellow you out. Lots of things I bet. Of course, I really don't want to do that, but if you leave me no choice..."

"Okay, okay," he muttered, starting to write quickly. He handed the script over.

Bingo. 250 5mgs.

Valium is a handy fog for a while, numbing your nerves, obscuring and bewildering but without giving much clarity. 15mgs are great with a couple of glasses of wine, besides.

They lasted all of two weeks, what with everyone asking me for them like they were Smarties. I say two weeks, but I was careful to keep a few back for me. I had grown accustomed to the fog, rather liked being in it and felt at a loss when cold, unfiltered reality entered my brain. Probably I was mildly addicted.

That weekend, I went up to my mate Dave's to smoke weed and listen to his hi-fi. His house, bought with the proceeds of an elaborate petrol coupon scam, was something of a drop in centre for the local stoners, a fact which pissed off his straight-laced girlfriend no end. She would sit in her separate plush living room, knitting and watching telly, while Dave played gabba techno at frightening volumes to the various waifs and strays who lolled about hallucinating.

On that particular night, Paul paid a visit. This was a guy who had just twelve months before felt at the top of his game controlling calls at the local call centre where half the young people in Stratford worked (the other half left town as soon as possible or end up working on tables). It seemed the pressure had been getting to him however, combined with an inheritance that he had converted into crack cocaine and, latterly, heroin, at the soonest available opportunity.

Tweedy was staggering when he arrived. Turns out he had been on methadone and Bacardi all day. But he did have a bottle of valium 10mgs on him, something we could appreciate.

I have a blank in my memory round about after the three pills I took kicked in. A floaty sensation that went on for I know not how long was interrupted by Dave shouting at Paul to wake up. I slowly came round to Dave, alternately picking up huge numbers of scattered green pills and going frantic that Paul had maybe died.

"Fuck, what do we do?" he asked.

"Well, you should really call him an ambulance," I said.

"No fucking way," said Dave, "If only I could drive-"

"You can't drive to the hospital," I said, "Not in your state."

"I meant just drive up the road somewhere and dump him," Dave said.

"Check his breathing," I said, grabbing a mirror from the wall. A white fog reassured us he wasn't about to throw a seven. We relaxed slightly, knowing that the task of picking up the pills could be done with less urgency.

When they were all up, and all evidence eliminated, the authorities were called.

The ambulance men knew Paul by name. He had done similar a few times before, always passing out at around the 100 milligram mark. A cry for help, I suppose.

At least he did it quietly.

Two nights later, Dave ignored him banging on his door, crying and shouting desperately that he was sorry and hoped he hadn't ruined their friendship. Not least of all because he didn't want to answer any questions about the missing valiums.

Paul ended up several months later being found OD'd in a ditch somewhere or something. I might be wrong.

Leicester 1998-1999.

The worst room I have ever stayed at was in Seymour Street, a road in Leicester's Highfields area, a notorious dump just at the back of the train station. Here, crack whores would strut their stuff on every corner and occasional race riots would kick off between the various communities jostling for space in this diseased and dilapidated neighbourhood.

I had taken up my cousin's offer of somewhere to stay after leaving Stratford-upon-Avon (under something of a cloud), and found myself in a cold and filthy annex off the part of the building in which he had his flat.

It had clearly been unused for many years when I went in; my cousin hadn't even bothered to check it out before cheerfully offering it to me.

A dark corridor led past a broken kitchen to a room covered with used tissues.

A grimy mattress lay on the floor next to two broken fridges.

A dark and sinister Victorian tallboy loomed threateningly next to a menacing wardrobe (incidentally, a tallboy is a piece of furniture- just wanted to clarify).

I was there eighteen months, my cousin and I's habit of both bankrupting ourselves every weekend made scraping a deposit together tricky.

We referred to it as the West Wing, rather grandly, despite the fact it was North-facing, its three exposed walls giving little protection from the outside cold.

Eventually the landlord found my stuff in there and figured I was squatting. The room was only supposed to be for my cousin to store his bike in. He wasn't allowed to sub-let.

"Right, well I want a hundred pounds a month off you," the landlord said. "I'm being very fair."

He was, he wasn't. It didn't stop my cousin still asking for the £250 each month for the privilege of living there. Christ, I could have got a flat in Highfields for less.

That room.

Let me tell you, I have never stayed in a room possessed by a more malevolent force than that place. I question why it had been abandoned all those years before.

Aside from a strange magical dream I had once on ketamine, the room was the setting for some extremely unwelcome manifestations during the night when my soul was at a low ebb.

My sister called these episodes sinkers. Generally occurring on the Tuesday evening after a heavy weekend, the sinkers came to me on quite a few occasions in that room in that flat.

I would be awake in the dark, yet not really awake- I was in my bed and yet unable to move. All I would be aware of was a feeling of incomparable terror and a heavy weight pinning me, stopping me from struggling.

Sometimes I would get free, stagger across the room to the light switch, but then the light wouldn't work, because I wasn't really awake at all- it was still this episode and I was deep in Sinkersville.

One night, I felt the usual paralysis, creeping dread, but there were voices shouting hateful things. My stereo starting blaring out, like the sound of a train whistle unbearably close.

“Shut up! Shut up! Shut up!” my astral self screamed, unable to turn the thing off because- well, this was astral world. Things like knobs and such work differently there. Or don’t work at all.

There was the sound of maniacal laughter, of the door repeatedly slamming. People kept running in and out of the room, approaching me with ghastly demonic faces.

My astral self struggled across the room, trying to wake up, but I couldn’t seem to do so.

“Fuck off!” I finally screamed. “Fuck off, you old cunt!”

And with that curse, the darkness lifted a little. I became slightly aware that I was actually in bed, trying like hell to wake up and out of this nightmare.

“Har, har, har!” a ridiculous pantomime pirate’s voice chuckled in my ear. “Fine words from a practicing Christian”

(I had prayed a couple of nights before- not something normally in my character, being English and agnostic. I was *that* desperate at the time).

The grip lifted more. I struggled awake.

“See you later, matey!” the voice chuckled nastily, disappearing into nothingness as I struggled back to reality.

*   *   *

I found after that that lighting a candle or sticking on some small electric light would banish these episodes. Light really did clear them away.

*   *   *

Many years later, having researched various esoteric strands, I have come to the conclusion that the visitation was some kind of djinni – or genie in English. It seems they like to hang about in disused and abandoned buildings, so the bedroom would have been an ideal lair. Until I turned up.

Not to be confused with the cuddly Disney / Robin Williams version, the djinn are very real entities who exist in a related dimension to ours, from which they can project themselves, latching onto us when we are fearful and at a low ebb. Some are bad, some are good, most are indifferent- much like people.

They are particularly adept at moving through the astral realm and so tend to appear to us in dreams, such as the one above.

JE SUIS
CRUSHED UP ASPIRIN AND
INFANT MILK FORMULA
makeyourselfuncomfortable.net

REGGIE ROLLY
HE FONDLES SHOPPING TROLLIES!
EE, I DON'T KNOW! YOU WAIT TEN MINUTES FOR A BUS AND NONE COME ALONG ALL AT ONCE!
AHA!
BUS STOP
EXCUSE ME, LUV - CAN I FONDLE YOUR SHOPPING TROLLEY?
EE! IT'S THAT NICE YOUNG MAN OFF THE TELLY!
SO -
OO! THERE MUST BE HALF A POUND OF CHEESE IN HERE!
?

Leicester, 1999.

I was sitting on the back bar in the main room of Club City, an unreconstituted seventies discotheque in a shabby district of Leicester, complete with lights in the floor and a carpet stained with thirty years of Carling Black Label, that had found a new lease of life thanks to the rave scene.

The bar I was sat on, at the back of the room, was closed for regular business that night and behind it were pitched a colourful clique of stoners and speed freaks who went under the collective name G.R.O.W.T.H. (Get Reality Over With, Take Hallucinogens), projecting warped visuals onto bed-sheets and blankets.

I grinned as I sat there coming up on a cheeky half, and looked over to Tommo who laughed like a lunatic. It would be a good night. The vibe was definitely there.

I looked round the room, taking it all in with my oversized eyes.

As I was nodding my head to the alien beats, a beer-bellied balding bloke, somewhere in his late thirties, sidled up and said "Hello mate. So, how many pills have you done tonight?"

That pulled me up sharp.

Even without the man's clunky conversational gambit, it was clear he was in intense discomfort. Waves of low-level fear and confusion seemed to radiate off him. I guessed he was CID.

I fixed him in the eye and, slowly and deliberately, said, "I don't take pills, actually."

At that, his mask collapsed and he reached out to me in panicky appeasement, stumbling over the words "Sorry mate, I'm an undercover policeman," before making a sudden exit out a nearby door.

"Wow. Freaky," I said, wondering if I should tell anyone. I scanned the crowd to see if there were any more suspicious characters in close proximity, but all I could make out were a load of young people on gurners, going bonkers and generally having a fine old time.

I turned to Tommo. "Can I have a word?"

"I tell you chap," he said, "I feel fucking fluffy tonight on these little uns, let me tell you."

"You'll never guess what just happened," I said, telling him what had happened.

"Fuck off," he said.

"Well, I found it a bit strange," I said. "An undercover copper telling me that that was what he was. It's kind of the last thing you'd want to do in his situation."

We let it go and went about our business- Tommo to tell people to keep their eyes peeled for unwelcome guests and me to go and dance by the bass bin for the next three hours.

When I had finally decided to go and have a bit of a sit down (about three pills later) I wandered out into the foyer where it was a bit cooler.

Sat round a table were four or five of my friends with this possible policeman from earlier, who was sat looking very interested as Monique, off her tits, was loudly telling him about all sorts of naughty stuff. She loved a good gossip really, and my friend from earlier was all ears.

He looked up as I approached and turned white then red, and sputtered a little before just about regaining his composure.

"So who's this you're talking to, Monique?" I asked, cutting in.

"Do you mind not interrupting me, hmmh?" Monique said crossly. "I'm in the middle of a story, actually."

"Do you know this man?" I said.

"Of course I do, Rick. His name's Bob and he works as a printer."

"Really? That's funny," I said. "He told me he was a policeman."

"Don't be ridiculous," said Monique.

"He did."

"No, he didn't."

"Yes, he did. He said he was a policeman. Didn't you?" I asked, sitting down with them and looking straight in his eyes.

He said, "That's stupid. Of course I didn't say that. I think you misheard me."

"No, you quite clearly said you were an undercover policeman, right before you vanished out the door."

"Then it was a joke," he said, getting up. He made his excuses.

After he was gone, Monique rounded on me. "Well, thank you for being so rude to my friend, Bob. Honestly, you can be vile with people."

"I was just repeating what he had said. And he didn't tell me he was a printer."

"Well, I can tell you he is," said Monique, getting all huffy.

Under sustained cross-examination, however, she was forced to concede that she had only just met him and so really had no way of knowing.

"But I still don't believe you," she said. "I think you must have been tripping out or something. You've got a weird sense of humour sometimes."

* * *

That night's After Hours was in the attic flat of Jon the No Longer Butcher, who had quit that cruel trade after an attack of guilt.

"I can't believe it, thinking back," he would say, shaking his head. "When I was a boy, I'd be hacking a cow in the neck with one hand, eating a beef sandwich with the other and all the while being sprayed head to foot with arterial blood."

Stories like this meant we were wary around Jon the No Longer Butcher, particularly when he got out his knife block, but his flat was somewhere to trash.

So I had been repeatedly telling my story about the policeman to anyone in the living room who would listen until I got yelled at to shut up because I was giving everyone the fear.

An uneasy hysteria was bubbling beneath the surface of the gathering and tensions began to build to the point where wild accusations about who was undercover rebounded round the walls.

"No, no, I didn't mean here," I said, trying to calm the situation. "It was back at the club!"

But the more I listened to the others the more I became convinced also that we had been infiltrated on our way out of the club, when about thirty of us had bundled ourselves in assorted minicabs and screeched off down the dual carriageway.

“Okay, okay, so we’ve been tailed,” I agreed. “This is obviously a sophisticated operation we’re dealing with.”

We ran through the most likely suspects. Finally, it came down to the black guy in the kitchen who had been wearing a beret, white gloves and dark glasses all night, despite telling us he was a chemistry student. Since being at Jon the No Longer Butcher’s, all he had done was this weird sort of robotic dance in the kitchen. Suspicious behaviour, we all agreed, not helped by the fact that none of us knew him.

We charged to the kitchen, Brian the Burglar in front, threatening to give him a hiding. My Big Gay Cousin took over, saying that he was an expert in getting people to talk.

“Who are you working for?” BGC bellowed, shaking the chemistry student by the scruff of his T shirt. “Who ARE you- really?”

When he roared, BGC was a terrifying sight: whether in drag or not. And he was still in drag at the After Hours, following a successful night of turning people away at the door of the house club, Hotdog. It made for a shocking scene. The poor student was terrified.

“I’m – I’m – I’m,” he gasped, “I’m Inspector…Morse.”

My cousin let go of him and he fell to the floor, choking.

“Well what do we do about it?” I said.

Brian the Burglar cut in. “I’ll handle this.”

He strode up to the man who was struggling to get to his feet and leaned over.

“Right, you can leave now,” he said. “You’re bringing everyone down.”

* * *

Even with Inspector Morse gone though, we all remained uneasy. There were three dealers there, at least one burglar and rogues in various shades of skulduggery. For my own part, I had shoplifted the occasional pack of razor blades (something I no longer do, I must add: due in large part to improved security measures).

"Who's a fucking policeman eh?" Jim kept repeating, pointing out people and chuckling nastily, until Brian the Burglar snapped.

"I'M the fucking policeman!" he shouted, leaping to his feet. "I'm the policeman. And you people are in a real spot of bother, I can tell you."

The room fell into astonished silence. Then my cousin piped up. "You? But that's ridiculous! Everyone knows you're a burglar!"

"And what better undercover disguise is there than that?" Brian the Burglar replied. "How on earth do you think I'm out on the streets, despite being known as Brian the Burglar to the whole of Leicester?"

These revelations were making us deeply uneasy. It seemed he was telling the truth.

"And I know all your businesses," he continued. "Intelligence gathering, we call it."

"Oh shit, look" I began, not knowing what to say, really. "Look, you know us. So you've been watching us all for a while. Then you know we're not bad people. I mean, evil. You know?"

"We don't want any trouble with the law," Jim said.

Brian the Burglar let out a nasty and sardonic laugh.

"You soft fucking twats," he sneered. "You really thought I was a policeman? How fucking insulting is that?"

time to

FACE FACTS:

1. It's that part of the head you look out of and eat with.
2. Everybody's got one. Some are nicer than others.
3. Yours, in particular, looks like a slapped arse.

B.L. SIBBUB
THE SON OF SATAN
AT SCHOOL -
BRIAN, KINDLY STOP SACRIFICING THAT SHEEP AND PAY ATTENTION TO YOUR SUMS.
2+2
= 4
PAH! THOU PIFFLING MORTAL! WHAT DO I NEED SUMS FOR WHEN I'M THE RULER OF THIS WORLD!?
LOOK, SHUT UP YOU LITTLE TWAT! I'M TAKING YOU UP TO THE HEAD FOR A SOUND WHACKING!
YOU BLOODY HUMAN!
WELL, YOUNG BRIAN, IT SEEMS YOU'VE BEEN A NAUGHTY BOY!
HAVE I? GOOD! DAD'LL BE PROUD!
HMM!

YES WELL I SPOKE TO YOUR FATHER ON THE PHONE AND HE RECOMMENDED I GIVE YOU A SEVERE SEEING TO, ADDING THAT YOU WERE A LOATHSOME LITTLE TURD!
SO BEND OVER WHILE I ROGER YOU SENSELESS WITH THIS FISHFINGER!
EEK!
ONE ROGERING LATER -
YOU'LL PAY FOR THIS! I'LL GET MY DAD ONTO YOU!
ONE ATTEMPTED BLACK MASS LATER -
SHIT! NOTHING'S HAPPENING!

HAST THOU FORSAKEN ME, SATAN MY FATHER?
DAMN! NO ANSWER! THE LINE MUST BE BUSY
SO-
HELLO-IS THAT CHILDLINE?
AND SO....
WHAT IS THE WORLD COMING TO?
THE CRIMES
HEADMASTER HELD IN SATANIC CHILD SEX ABUSE

And so Rolf Harris is finally bang to rights for being a nonce and I for one am very glad indeed.

You see- in 1981, when I was aged only eight, Rolf Harris very nearly ruined my life.

It was my parents' fault, of course.

They had taken me on a pre-Christmas trip to the local Cash & Carry: a kind of trade warehouse for small businesses (such as our pub) where you could buy industrial-sized blocks of cheese and the like. In my family, this pretty much counted as a day out.

As it was Christmas time, in addition to the cheese, chips and glacé cherries, the Cash & Carry was also stocking various albums. Being a bit of a home computer fan (I had a VIC-20 at the time, with a whopping 3.5K of usable RAM) my eyes were instantly drawn to the cover of Kraftwerk's Computer World. They were also fascinated by the cover of Pink Floyd's Dark Side of the Moon.

Immediately, I asked my mum if I could please please please have both, or either (I wasn't greedy) for Christmas.

"Oh, you don't want THOSE!" she cackled at me. "You wouldn't like THOSE at all! They're just a LOAD of RUBBISH!"

"But pl-e-e-e-a-se!" I pleaded.

"Oh, come along," she said, pulling me by my coat.

I kept wailing "Pl-e-e-e-a-se!" all the way to the car, until she snapped "If you don't stop whingeing you won't be getting ANYTHING for Christmas! ...except a BLOODY SMACK!"

I took this to mean a remote but possible yes to Kraftwerk and/or Pink Floyd.

I could but hope.

* * *

Later that day found us in Woolworths, where I was suspiciously waylaid by dad at the pick'n'mix. Either by chance or malicious design, we both ended up at the tills at exactly the same time as mum. She hadn't seen me, so I got a good view of a cassette tape she was holding.

Even at a distance, I could see the plastic case was wrapped in the tell-tale cardboard of the Music For Pleasure label. Although I was only eight, I already knew that they released nothing but crap, sold cheaply in Woolies.

Closer, I got a look at the cover.

It was Rolf Harris Sings Songs for Children.

"Who's that for?" I asked.

"Oh, er.. well," mum began. "It's for a very special little boy for his Christmas present."

"Oh," I replied, blankly.

I didn't know any very special little boys. But maybe it was for my one of my cousins.

* * *

Of course, Christmas arrived and I opened up the Rolf tape and felt a great wave of despair at the family I had been born into. Not for the first time, I hoped that I was maybe adopted and might therefore be rescued by my real parents. The ones who understood me.

*   *   *

A few years later, I managed to buy both Dark Side of the Moon and Computer World (on CD by then) and they remain two of my all-time favourite albums.

As for the Rolf tape- after one cursory listen, I pulled half the tape out and made out that my tape player had chewed it up.

I didgerididn't like him then and I didgeridon't now.

INSPURASHNUL KWOTS

"Personally, I think porn is disgusting. But only after I have cum. Then, I'm not sure which I wipe first- my browsing history or my belly, with an old, grey gym sock."

- J.R.R. Tolkein

"I quite often think that life is pretty good, actually. But only when I'm drunk, on holiday or on hardcore drugs."

- C.S. Lewis

"I would love to fuck the system. But there's so many holes in it I have option paralysis"

- J.R. Hartley

WACKY
SPONSORED BY SANDOLIN®
KRAZYBALLS

FLIPPING HECK! TIME TO ENJOY SOME OF MY FAVOURITE SNACK!
TUNE IN WITH
GLEN COINLID
HA HA HA MR. KRAZYBALLS! THERE'LL BE NO FRUIT PASTILLES FOR YOU!
EEK! IT'S ST. DINSMARG!
YES IT IS I – THE HALF-MAN, HALF-BIRD, HALF-TAPLEN FILE AND I HAVE EATEN YOUR SWEETIES!
YOU...YOU... MONSTER!
I AM NO MONSTER AND TO PROVE IT...HERE...HAVE ONE OF MY EXTRA-CHEWY TOFFEES!
WELL... OKAY...

SO-
OO FIDDLESTICKS! I'VE CRACKED A TOOTH!
NOT TO WORRY, MR. KRAZYBALLS! WE SIMPLY TIE ONE END OF THIS STRING TO THE TROUBLESOME TOOTH...
MFFGGKXXM!
...AND THE OTHER TO THIS DOOR KNOB, AND THEN WE MERELY...
TUNE IN WITH
GROOVY!
...SLAM!
SCHLOP!
RON GRIDCHARTS

It's been a while since I last did ketamine, but I hear it's still in use by the feral yoof of the UK.

It used to be used as a battlefield anaesthetic for humans, but got canned after the Vietnam War due to the nightmarish hallucinations it could spawn for people lost in the jungle with their legs blown off.

The effects of ketamine vary enormously with the dosage.

If you take a small amount, it gives you a warm, floaty buzz, like you're paddling in the shallows of something terribly strange. It can even get you up and dancing.

If you take some more (and you may as well, there's loads left) then you get a weird feeling like someone is opening up all your mental filing cabinets and chucking the contents all around your head. Your vision goes square almost, and you start to become dissociated from your body. If you try to get up and walk, though, you can do it in a single bound. Congratulations. You are now a pod person.

Sniffing more and things get really weird. The dimensions resize before losing their function as you slip

down

the

h

o

l

e

*   *   *

One night I took some before going to bed. I slipped off quickly enough, but instead of dreaming, I found myself in my astral form, in an astral version of my room. I could see my real self, asleep in the bed, and tried to reconnect. However, I slipped through the bedclothes instead and down through layers of velvety darkness.

I climbed out of the sky and down to the ground, looking about me. I seemed to be backstage somewhere, with various people running about with bits of scenery and equipment.

A woman with a clipboard approached. She wasn't quite human.

"What are you doing?" she said. "You're not supposed to be around here."

"Sorry," I said, "I wasn't aware of that."

"Well, this is a restricted area. It's off-limits to dreamers." She got closer, inspecting me. "Wait a minute, you're not dreaming are you?"

"No, I've taken something."

"You've been doing ketamine, haven't you?" she demanded.

"Yes," I said, expecting a reprimand, but none came. So I said, "Look, while I'm here, do you think you could show me around?"

She said yes.

It seems I had ended up stuck somewhere in the production process of dreams, wandering around like I was on a movie lot or something. The woman showed me towards what looked like a swimming pool, overlaid with a rubber sheet. On this various strange creatures bounced up and down in lanes.

"What are they doing?" I asked.

"They're practicing holding on," she said. "People think they have to struggle to hold onto their dreams, and that's partly right. But dreams also have to work at holding onto people."

We walked on through municipal corridors piled high with boxes. (Backstage, dreamland is a bit shabby really. You get something similar at theatres and TV studios.)

It was then that I became aware of being hunted. A group of guards or something had spotted me and were closing in. In response to the danger, I raised my consciousness level, floating up back towards my room and a waking state.

And a cigarette.

My second arrest was in 1999. Exactly like my first it was for possession of a single gramme of hashish, street value about £3. It wasn't even good hash. It was soap bar, so they had a cheek arresting me really. Everyone knows there is little to no THC in soap- that's why they stopped selling it. It's all 'head cheese' these days, apparently, and the cheesier the better.

My friend, let's call him Charles (because that was his name), had a problem at the time with hard drugs (I try not to be judgemental, but watch out for junkies, basically). I happened to be with him when he needed to score- after a club when we had both done pills. I was dubious, but as he was clucking at the time (i.e. withdrawing), I kept my mouth shut. I needed a lift home after all and it was cold outside.

We drove in his car up to the Braunstone Estate, past tower blocks whose shuttered windows were like broken teeth and into a cul-de-sac where we pulled up next to a garage.

Immediately a guy was at Charles' window and a deal was made. He slipped away into the shadows.

"Thank fuck for that," Charles was saying, turning the keys in the ignition.

At that moment, in front of us brightened up considerably. A flashing blue light threw shadows across the wall.

"Uh oh," I said as my car door was opened from the outside.

All the usual bollocks, but they only searched the car due to the fact that Charles had an out of date tax disc. Turns out he was disqualified from driving also, plus had an outstanding conviction for some fine or other he had never paid.

So we both got taken to the station by the officers, and I was expecting to have to go through the same kind of fascistic shit that the cops in Birmingham had pulled on me.

"So, you had any previous dealings with the police?" one asked after I had been charged with possession and told I was going to be cautioned.

"Yeah, yeah- I have, as a matter of fact," I said, totally pissed off. "I was arrested and given a three year caution for possession of one gramme of marijuana just over three years ago!"

The irony of this wasn't lost on the police, who started laughing like it was hilarious.

"Yeah, very funny officers," I said. "This might be some big joke to you, but you know what you've done to me tonight? You've turned me into a criminal. You've criminalised me by arresting me for something innocuous and everyday. How do you think that makes me feel?"

They looked puzzled. Obviously empathy didn't play a huge part in police training back in the day. I'm sure it still doesn't.

"Is it any wonder that nobody of my generation," I continued, warming to my theme,"has anything other than contempt for the police and the Rule of Law, when you marginalise and criminalise perfectly law-abiding citizens like this?"

At this, they crumpled.

"Oh, shit," one said."Look, sorry mate- we really didn't mean to pull you."

They both were really worried, for some reason.

"That's right mate," the other said, "We can tell you're a good chap. We really didn't expect to pick up someone like you. Not in Braunstone."

"Well, you did. What now?" I asked.

Instead of being fingerprinted and grilled, I was taken down to the cells while they processed my details. This usually takes four hours or more, so I was surprised when they came to let me out after only an hour.

"Okay, you'll be free in a minute," the officer said. "The duty sergeant just wants a quick word with you before you go."

"Fine," I said.

The sergeant, when I saw him, smiled in an ingratiating way, obviously embarrassed.

"Look, I just wanted to say that, if you get stopped by the police again, and they ask you if you've ever had dealings with the police before," here his voice dropped, becoming almost conspiratorial: "Tell them- tell them you don't know. Say you can't remember. All right?"

Afterwards, the officer who had arrested me drove me back to my doorstep, which was nice.

In the car he said, "You're a graduate, aren't you?"

"Yeah," I said. "Drama and English."

"I'm a graduate too," he said. "Chemistry. I suppose you're now wondering why I'm in the police, aren't you?"

I wasn't, but to humour him I said "Why?"

"Well, you know how it is. Met a nice girl. Wanted to settle down. Have kids. No jobs in Leicester. It pays well."

I could understand. "It's not an easy place to make a life really, is it?" I said.

"No, Leicester's not a very nice place. Where are you from?"

"Stratford-Upon-Avon."

"Bit of a culture shock coming here then, I suppose."

"Maybe," I said. "I lived for two years on Seymour Street, with the prostitutes and the crack dens and the gangsters and all the inner city pond life Leicester can muster. And you know what?"

"No. What?" the policeman asked, glancing at me.

"I had respect. These people- who are from a completely different background- they got to know me. And they respected me. I was looked up to in that neighbourhood. You know?"

We drove in silence after that.

That was meant to just be a sneaky fart there. But I think I've actually followed through.

After three years of Leicester, I finally got it together enough to move to my sister's in Bath. She had a good job at the time in publishing and I thought maybe she could help hook me up with something. Besides, after visiting the place on and off for a couple of years, I was falling for its Regency charms.

My sister had insisted in advance that staying at hers would be strictly for as long as it took me to find work and digs and I assured her that I would want to get out of her hair pretty quickly also. Her wrath, when aroused, could be a downright scary thing, and her spare room was already fit to bursting with her boyfriend's records and decks and Star Wars figurines. My mum and step-dad drove me down with my stuff. We were starting afresh after not talking for over a year due to a letter I had written and posted, whilst on acid, in which I had formally resigned from being her son. I had had my reasons.

Helping me move was a goodwill gesture and I was a happy beneficiary, free at last from the smoking factory chimneys and chav bars of the East Midlands.

My first job was a non-starter: freelance travel writer for some internet start-up that folded in its first month. Then an agency called me with a two-week booking answering the telephone and giving some spiel at a mortgage brokers. I said yes.

The weekend before I started, one of my sister's ne'er-do-well friends- Mad Rachel- talked me into bleaching the grade three haircut I had been giving myself ever since getting hold of some clippers. It would make me look more distinctive, she said. But everywhere I went, strangers would point and grin, saying "Fucking hell, it's Eminem!"

* * *

The first morning of my mortgage job, I was shown up to the enormous open-plan goldfish bowl office of the mortgage brokers by one of the case handlers, who turned me over to the MD who chained me to a desk not far from his. As he gave me my brief, I was aware of being the focus of most of the staff's attention.

"What's Eminem doing here?" I heard one say.

I sighed. It would be a long two weeks.

The MD filled me in. Management buyout. Hadn't trained sufficient staff to handle the calls. Wanted me to take a few details. Tell them I wasn't advising, but Halifax had the best rate and if they wanted to look at it I'd get something in the post. Nothing too strenuous. Not after ringing up harassed IT managers for eighteen months and trying to engage them in a chat about flood wiring.

Turned out the MD was listening in on my calls. Soon the Sales Manager took an interest, then the Sales Director. Within three days they had asked me into a private meeting.

"How is it that someone with your obvious abilities is temping?" the MD asked.

"I've just moved here," I said.

"Would you be interested in something permanent?" the Sales Director said.

"It's good for morale- having Eminem on the team," the Sales Manager said, chuckling.

"Sure. Why not," I said. It would get me out from my sister's.

* * *

The interview was a joke. The Sales Manager leaned back in his chair with his arms behind his head and his feet on the table.

"Yeah yeah. That's cool. That's cool," he said. "We reckon you could sell ice to the Eskimos."

"Innuit," I said.

"Sorry?"

"I said 'I know it'". (I didn't want him to twig at this stage that I was a smart arse.)

"Just one last question," he said. "It's a formality, really. I don't suppose you've any dodgy credit history? Unpaid bills? That sort of thing."

I told him I'd need a pen and some paper. A4 size.

They got back to me the next day with a printout from Experian. No record of my defaults, which was a real surprise.

"But we can't have you giving financial advice, I'm afraid," said the SD. "Company rules."

"Instead we'd like to offer you a marketing position," said the MD. "Execution only. You chase up the leads the advisors aren't interested in."

I said ok. What else could I do?

* * *

My sister was delighted and so was her boyfriend. Finally, he'd have room to display his Death Star. I bought some shirts from Marks & Sparks and threw myself into house hunting.

I hadn't thrown myself very long or far (just to the nearest pub) when my friend Orange said there was probably a room going at the house he was staying at.

"How do you mean- probably?" I asked.

"Well, it's the landlord's room but he says he's moving out."

"Sounds good. When can I see it?"

By divine providence, the landlord was in the same pub at the time. Which shows even divine providence can be a crock of shit.

His name was Barry. He was a chubby and cheerful black guy who spoke with a strong West Country burr and worked as Art Director for an aviation magazine. He grinned and grinned, clapping his arm around my shoulder and saying "Welcome to my home. We're one big happy family, isn't that right Orange?"

"Err. Yeah," said Orange. "I'm just going to the bar."

* * *

The next day found me in front of Barry's poky semi-detached on Foxhill, ringing the doorbell while my sister's boyfriend waited in his car with my stuff.

The door was answered by a mouth-breathing gangly youth with a vacant look about him.

"Hi," I said. "I'm Rick."

"Right…?"

"I'm moving in."

"Are you?"

"Yes. I spoke to Barry earlier."

"Oh. He's not in."

"Yeah, I know he's not. I phoned him. He said someone would be at home."

"Oh. Right."

He stood in the doorway shuffling from one foot to the other, unsure of what to do next.

"So can I come in?" I asked.

"Oh. yeah. Right. Sure."

He stepped aside.

"What's your name?" I asked.

"Alan."

"Nice to meet you, Alan. So- where's the room?"

"What room?"

"To put my stuff in."

"Err." His gaze glazed over.

"Okay, tell you what. I'll put it in the kitchen till Barry gets back."

It wasn't until I had finished stacking everything in the kitchen that I noticed something odd about its ceiling. Specifically, a huge gaping hole with the bottom of a bath poking through. I told myself that living here was going to be strictly short-term.

Around six, Orange showed up.

"What's going on with the bath?" I asked.

"Yeah, Barry says he's getting it fixed," he replied.

"Which room's mine? I haven't been upstairs yet."

"Okay, I'll show you."

As we climbed the stairs, Orange said, "Now, technically the room's yours but Barry hasn't moved his stuff out yet. He's still looking for accommodation."

"So where's he going to sleep?"

"Dunno. Sofa probably. You'll have to ask him."

"How are you finding it here, Orange?" I asked.

"Oh, it's okay. Barry's cool. Just one thing I didn't mention."

"What's that?"

"Well, Barry's a great guy. Just one detail I forgot to tell you."

"Which is?"

"Well..."

We were in the room by now and Orange lowered his voice so that Alan, downstairs, wouldn't hear. "He's got a massive problem with crack cocaine."

"Oh. Great."

* * *

About eight, Barry got back. I was sat in the living room with Orange and Alan, watching Eastenders or some such crap, when he walked in.

"Alan!" he shouted. "Why's the washing up not done?"

"Oh right. Sorry," Alan said, cringing as he slunk off to the kitchen.

"Rick!" he beamed. "You moved in all right?"

"Yeah. Well, my stuff's in the kitchen."

"Right."

"I didn't know where to put it. There's all your stuff in the wardrobe and cupboards."

"Only temporary." He flopped down on the sofa. "Soon be on the move. I can clear some space."

"Okay, that's cool," I said.

"In the meantime, I'll crash on the sofa at night. Is that okay with you two?"

"Sounds fine by me," I said.

"Sure," said Orange, nodding his assent.

"Alan!" shouted Barry out to the kitchen. "Make us all a cup of tea!"

Turning to us, he gave a conspiratorial aside. "Nice lad, but a bit dim."

I asked what Alan's story was. Barry told me he had found him sleeping rough, a situation he had been in for three years since running away from a foster home. He had spent some time on the streets of London before hitch-hiking to Bath, hoping to meet up with an old friend of his. Only trouble was that he didn't have his friend's address and hadn't run into him, so he had ended up alternating between sleeping in a homeless shelter and under a railway arch, which was where Barry had spotted him.

"He's just a kid," Barry explained. "I didn't want him getting mixed up in drugs or anything, so I took him in."

"That's a kind thing to do," I said.

"Sometimes, mateys, you gotta do the right thing. Incidentally, you don't have your rent money on you by any chance?"

"Sure."

"Only I've a friend coming round I owe some to, and I'm a bit short myself at the moment."

"No problem."

"Alan!" roared Barry. "Where's this cup of tea then?"

* * *

At half nine, the doorbell rang.

"Right, that's my mate. Alan- go to your room."

Alan got up and left for his room- if that's what you can call the cupboard under the stairs that houses the electricity meters. Barry opened the front door and showed his guest in.

"This is Zee," he said.

"Hi Zee," I said.

Zee grunted and sank into the armchair, where he sat moodily picking his teeth.

Barry said, "Look, guys, I've got something personal I want to talk to Zee about. Do you think you could go upstairs for a bit?"

Orange and I got up and left.

* * *

In his room, I asked Orange about Zee.

"Jamaican yardie. Barry's dealer. Only we're not supposed to know," Orange said as he mixed two house tunes together.

"I didn't get a good vibe off him."

"No-one ever does."

About five minutes later, Barry was knocking on the door. I let him in. He was carrying a crack pipe.

"Look, here's the story," he said. "Zee has offered to give us a rock each for free."

"Really?" I said.

"Yeah. Good of him, right?"

"I guess."

"So, just one house rule. Alan's not to know about any of this. Nor anyone else in town. I've a reputation to keep."

"Your secret is my secret," I said.

"No worries," said Orange.

"Good," said Barry, fiddling with the pipe. "And as a little house warming, I want you to have first lick."

* * *

The mechanics of crack are that it's instantly addictive, but for that night only. You can go to bed and forget about it the next day- if you can go to bed. Its nature means that as soon as you exhale it, you're wanting another hit. You watch the pipe being passed around, wondering irritably when and if you're going to get another toot.

Zee's free stone was nothing of the sort. As soon as it was gone we pooled our cash and gave it to Barry to go down and get more. And when that was gone we were ordering a taxi to drive us down to the cash point.

* * *

The next evening, as I painfully climbed the three uphill miles from work to Foxhill because I didn't have the bus fare home, I meditated on my financial foolishness the night before.

It was some mantra.

* * *

Life at Barry's was pretty surreal. His brother was a respected drum & bass DJ and producer who never visited. Instead, his brother's ex-girlfriend came round twice a week to make sure we were all eating properly. Barry would cook jerk chicken, which we'd have with red wine out in the garden.

Twice a week also, Zee would pay a visit which he spent sat watching TV and communicating in grunts while Alan was banished to his cupboard and the rest of us to Orange's room. Various friends would visit on these evenings until it became a regular full-blown crack session.

Now, I'm a sober, respectable and upstanding guy and what had started as a novelty was quickly becoming a royal pain. My walks up the hill had developed a depressing regularity that the stunning scenery did little to dispel. Particularly with Foxhill as my destination.

The house Barry was moving to fell through and soon all talk of him moving out was a memory. What didn't fall through, thankfully, was the bath in the kitchen ceiling- although its angle had shifted alarmingly over time. Water collected in the far end from the plughole and only the brave or foolhardy would countenance anything more than the briefest of showers in it.

Alan got a job at KFC which made Barry happy as it meant more money for rocks. Then he lost it due to incompetence, which sent Barry wild.

He had been taking more and more time off from his job at the aviation magazine- justifying it at first by saying he had a great team under him and they could all cope on their own now and then, that things were flying high. When he got a final warning, however, it was clear that his autopilot had been knocked out. He was now entering a terminal descent phase.

I had problems of my own at the mortgage brokers. They thought I was a right weirdo.

"Some of the advisors think you're a right weirdo," laughed the Sales Director in a private room. "Not me of course. Ha ha."

"I'm just different is all. I'm not so money-motivated," I said.

"So what the bloody hell are you doing working at a mortgage brokers, then?"

He had a point. All the directors of the company- the ones who had bought it out- were worth over ten million pounds each. The Chairman was worth a staggering 140 million, made by taking a cut from the investments of others. Weapons and oil stocks mostly.

The guilt he felt from this, together with his relaxed schedule, gave him the time and moral incentive to get into green campaigning. Together with Greenpeace, he set up the Stop Esso campaign (Exxon Mobil in the US), which was ironic because there was an Esso garage right next door to the office where most of the staff filled up on sandwiches and petrol.

I sent him an email congratulating him on his Stop Esso venture. I said I thought it was a great idea. I said I had signed the petition (I didn't have a car, so it was no great shakes). I said I was proud to be working for someone with morals. I suppose he could afford them.

After that, he made a point of coming over to my desk pretty regularly for a chat about green issues or organic farming, something that didn't go unnoticed by the rest of the staff. I covered my space with anarchist slogans and peace signs. I installed an Eminem screensaver. Fuck it.

My direct marketing campaign was beginning to go very well. I chased and chased and chased even the smallest lead, practically guaranteeing they would sign. We didn't charge them. It could only save them money. We knew the best deals at any given time. The bank (whichever was flavour of the week) got a new customer, we got 250 quid from the bank.

Then mutters of discontent from the advisors reached my ears. They wanted to know what the bloody hell I was doing to convert so many leads.

It was simple really. I was just calling people back. The advisors, by contrast, were so lazy and money-grubbing that they wouldn't bother shifting for anything less than a million pound mortgage. They'd send the pack and that would be that. The pack would hang around the prospect's in-tray or mantelpiece for a week or so before being chucked in the trash. That's how it is. I followed up each and every one of my leads and got a success rate double that of almost all of the advisors. It wasn't hard to see what was coming.

Rates settled down. It became unfashionable to switch mortgages- far better to settle into a long-term fixed rate. Calls into the company started drying up.

There was a big meeting to which I wasn't invited where the advisors demanded all the leads I was working on.

"Sorry Rick," said the Marketing Manager. "It's above my head."

"I understand that."

"Also, as we were building towards a three month pipeline and the project has been pulled after eleven weeks, I'm afraid we can't give you any commission for the leads you've generated."

This is how directors get to be so rich, I suppose. Crapping on the little guy.

I got given a new role as Buy-To-Let Assistant to a guy who didn't want or need my assistance. He preferred to be stressed out on his own.

I was told to just sit at my desk and keep myself busy. It was about then that I developed my surfing habit. I learnt about the NWO, the Bilderberg, the Trilateral Commission, the Freemasons and Schnews and grassroots activism. I ended up going on a march to the G8 conference in Genoa. I felt I was doing my bit. Meanwhile, the advisors were all busy whingeing about having all these shitty leads to chase. Some people are never happy.

* * *

One night I got home to find Alan alone in the house, in the living room, in the dark.

"Hi Alan. Why's it so dark?"

Alan looked startled by the revelation that it was, indeed, dark.

"Oh yeah," he said. "It happened so slowly I didn't really notice."

He looked lost. I turned on the lights. Then I turned on the TV.

"Yeah, right," he said. "That's better."

Soon after Barry got home. He looked both furious and scared, which is no mean feat.

"Sorry mateys. The house is being repossessed," he blurted out.

It turned out he had been spending the mortgage money on crack.

"And I've been fired."

He started to say something else, but the sound was obliterated by the most almighty crash from the direction of the kitchen. The ceiling had finally given way under the weight of the bath and the gallons of water in it that nobody had bothered to bale out.

Barry shuffled out of the living room in a daze, Alan and I following behind.

Plaster and wrecked building materials lay everywhere and dust fell thickly through the gaping hole, now kitchen-sized. Water was pissing a cascade down the wall.

Barry didn't say anything. He seemed to have lost the capacity for words. I broke the silence.

"The latest in open plan living, eh?" I said.

"Does this mean I have to move out?" asked Alan.

BERTIE BLEEP
- HE SHAGS SHEEP
NO, I DON'T!
BAAA
CHRIST ALL-BLOODY-MIGHTY! LOOK AT ALL THAT RED-HOT CRUMPET!
FWOR!
BAAAAAAA
I CAN HARDLY CONTROL MYSELF! I JUST BETTER PUT [redacted] MY...

...VELCRO GLOVES ON? SHIT! I'VE LOST THEM! OH! MY GOD!
WELL, I BETTER GO AND SEE IF THE VILLAGE STORES HAVE ANY...
TO VILLAGE
AT THE SHOP
NO I'M AFRAID WE SOLD THE LAST FIFTY PAIRS TO THE BRITISH GOATSHAGGING ASSOCIATION ONLY YESTERDAY SORRY, MR. BLEEP
MAN URE
TCH! HOW AM I GONNA GET MY END AWAY NOW
? ?
EXCUSE ME

BUT I AM A REFORMED SEXUAL PERVERT AND I WONDER IF YOU WOULD LIKE THIS PAIR OF VELCRO GLOVES?
CORKS!
NOW TO GO AND SEE FLOSSIE!
BUT—
HUNH? WHERE'S SHE GONE?
GONE
YOO HOO! FARMER NUTTER! WHERE HAVE ALL YOUR SHEEP GONE?
EH?
OO AR! ELLO YOUNG BERTIE! OIVE BEEN TO MARKET AND OIVE SOLD EM ALL FOR MEAT
EEK!

OH POOR FLOSSIE! I LOVED HER SO!
SOB!
I SUPPOSE I BETTER GO HOME, THEN. THERE'S ;SOB; NOTHING MORE FOR ME HERE
SNIF
OH, HELLO! DEAR! I'VE MADE YOU A NICE DINNER....
OH?
...LAMB STEAKS!
EEEP!

April 2002, and a bullet list of where I was at, was

- Bath

- Staying temporarily in my sister's spare room

-J obless

- Nearly broke, having spent almost all my savings on a six month doss around Thailand.

Unlike my previous arrival in Bath, where I had soon found somewhere to work- at a mortgage brokers; and somewhere to live- in a crack house, this trying to return to Bath after six months away was proving problematic. Testing the waters of the job market, things were tepid at best.

Instead of just falling into something, I was being offered scraps of temporary work on zero hour contracts, something which is apparently very much a feature of British life these days.

These jobs had included

- Transferring one of Future Publishing's many magazines about PCs onto the internet, cutting and pasting article after article, pic by pic: we eventually ran out of back issues

- Sanitarium Kitchen Porter: I thought the guy was being a bit patronising

- Insurance Company Mail Room Assistant: the regular guy came back

- Freelance Travel Writer: the company it was for pulled the plug on the whole project the day I submitted my first article

- Casual Labourer: which was very infrequent

All in all, it wasn't going anywhere, really.

My sister's insistence that "I really love you but you need to move out soon because you're starting to piss me off" was fair enough.

The agency who were getting me most of these gigs were super positive that something would come through and to hold tight. My recruiter was a young woman called Kirstie, who had a warm and flirtatious manner, together with a seeming glee in throwing anything and everything at me.

"You're one of our star temps, Rick," Kirstie said. "And I *believe* in you."

- – -

What *I* believed that April day was that in a way it was a good thing I had no work to go to as it was my birthday, but also rather a pisser that no work meant no income.

Despite this, I had unenthusiastically suggested a meal at an Italian restaurant and twelve or so people had agreed to come.

So I was sat having a quick beer or two at The Porter before the meal, when there was a knocking and waving at the window. It was the beaming face of Teardrop Lee (named because of his facial tattoo), his features curiously twisted in the warped, old panes.

He rushed into the pub- a mad and noisy entrance in which he theatrically gurned before spitting out the joke teeth he was wearing. Following a few "Hello, mate!" salutations, delivered at frightening volume, he then put on a pair of joke glasses- the ones with eyeballs on springs- which boinged and bounced to maximum comic effect.

"Oh, hi Lee," I said. "How's it going?"

I told him it was my birthday. At that, he took it up a notch by ordering four whiskies, four pints and two shots for us to share, before bundling me into the toilets with a wrap of cocaine and an ecstasy tablet. When I got back he forced my mouth open and threw another tablet in. "For good measure."

We hadn't even reached the end of the booze when I began to feel decidedly fucked. Teardrop Lee had matched me in intake and was getting crazier by the minute.

For some reason, I then thought it would be a good idea to invite him along to the Italian restaurant, so we both staggered up the road to the meal together.

I was a bit late, to be honest, which is never a good thing to be in England.

My sister's sour visage hove into view. My vision was being rapidly agitated by the pill- an experience known as chuckle vision- but still, it was definitely her. And she was definitely, thoroughly pissed off with me.

Eleven other people- all friends who had wanted to come share my birthday with me in a low-key midweek kind of way, were sat round the table. They had been waiting for me before ordering.

And (quick tense change here) even though I know these are people who like me very much, I'm not picking up on any of that love right now. Quite the opposite.

I go to take my seat when my sister hisses at me "And what time do you call this?" but I don't reach it before Teardrop Lee makes his entrance.

Topping even his bravura performance at the Porter earlier, this time he simply sails in with a flying kick down the stairs leading to the table, which is in a lower section to the entrance. He's whooping as he does this.

There is the most almighty crash as the table- which it turns out is only a cheap fold-up one beneath the posh tablecloth- collapses completely, smashing on peoples' knees and with all the glasses, cutlery, plates and condiments going flying.

There is a shocked silence throughout the restaurant as Lee manages to pick himself up- a silence so complete that even the furthest table hears his stage-whispered instruction to me to "Go and snort a fat line of this coke in the toilets. I'll deal with this."

I could swear I heard shouting as I was doing so, and indeed I could.

When I staggered out again, my sister was screaming at Lee that he was a fucking wanker and what the fuck did he think he was doing.

"Sorry, I went a bit too far that time," Lee was saying. He put in his false teeth and he put on his boingy eyes but nobody was having it.

I thought I could make the situation calmer by wading in with "Hey, hey! It's my birthday and Lee's my guest!" which my sister took very badly, exploding in the kind of rage-fuelled response she is periodically capable of.

It is a response that means it is time to move out.

Her anger unabated, we managed to sit around a hastily replaced table. My menu came.

Lee wandered off to the bar and ordered a drink. "Nah, couldn't eat a thing," he slurred. "Far too fucked."

I looked at the menu which had no appeal for me either.

"Do you know, I think I'll just have a drink at the bar as well," I said.

This caused a bigger uproar, as those who had been quiet up until now suddenly rounded on me.

"Fucking hell mate, it's just totally out of order. You keep us waiting for half an hour and you turn up in that state. What the fuck are you thinking?"

Looking around the restaurant to see if there were any supportive faces at all- there were none- I noticed the couple on the next table from ours for the first time. But when I looked over, I realised that they had been glaring at me for some time.

Sat in a stunned silence of spilt soy sauce was Kirstie from the recruitment agency, together with a man who looked very much like a client.

There was some kind of paperwork on their table- a contract, perhaps, now sadly splashed with splats of something from when Lee had broken the table.

Kirstie spoke. I had nothing.

"Having a nice birthday are we, Richard?" she asked, coldly.

- – -

The next morning, I was on the eight o'clock train to London, unsure of anything very much beyond the following:

- I had two-thousand pounds in the world

- I had a room with friends in a place called Wandsworth for one month only

- I had never been to Wandsworth before

- I had never been in London that much before

- I could be making either a very good or very bad move here

- Or it could, of course, just be mediocre.

In the event, it was mainly mediocre.

But that is another story and shall be told another time.

Sometimes, I actually poo myself when I'm on stage. It's not really an artistic statement. I just never got very good toilet training.
-Lady Gaga
makeyourselfuncomfortable.net

THE BRAIN FRAZZLING ADVENTURES OF
NORRIS SMITH
(A BANK MANAGER)
AND A LUNATIC
GOOD LORD! IT SAYS HERE IN THE PAPER THAT THE LOCAL MENTAL HOME IS CLOSING DOWN!
SPORT
CLOSED DOWN? BUT I WAS COMMITTED TO THAT!
WHAT ME WORRY?

And so I got spewed up onto the streets of Wandsworth, South London with my suitcase wheels clicking and clacking over the cracks in the pavement.

It was plain to see, within seconds of getting to London, that the streets were not paved with gold at all, despite what some massive Dick had once claimed. Instead, they were spattered with black chewing gum stains, spat out greenies and the occasional dog turd.

Menacing teenagers were slumped in sulky gangs outside the Arndale Centre and the jammed traffic belched black fumes all the way back to Clapham.

Not sure of which direction to take, I pulled out my Nokia to call my friend Orange, whose spare room I was about to reside in for a period of up to one month.

As well as a suitcase, I had with me a small rucksack which contained three ounces of the West Country's finest skunk weed. I figured I could maybe supplement whatever income I managed to rustle up in London with a spot of low-level weed dealing. And because I have consistently been incapable of following the advice to 'never get high off your own supply', all of the following should be taken as a work of fiction, pieced together from the scraps of detritus my brain managed to hold onto during my time in the capital.

* * *

"Well, good to have you here, mate," Orange was saying, offering me a line of coke. "But now you *are* here, what are you gonna *do*?"

"I'm still working on that bit," I said, snorting. "I'll sort something out."

"Yeah, yeah," said Orange. "London's full of opportunities. Only it's also full of people jostling to take them."

* * *

And so it was, looking in Loot, that I managed to fall into a job answering the telephone at Reuters, a position I would remain in for two years. The job was boring yet not stressful enough to warrant quitting- paying enough to put up with it, yet not enough to allow me ambition to think beyond the next pay day.

It had its advantages. At 7p.m. you were on your own- which meant locking the security door until the 11pm switchboard person came on. On the night shift you were alone until 7a.m. The phone would ring maybe three or four times in the night and then you'd have to do something. Otherwise, it was just sleeping on the sofa, smoking, watching TV and drinking the odd beer (or six).

The week of nights meant being driven to work along the Embankment by an Addison Lee BMW or similar, whose regular drivers would pin me down into spilling the beans on what was really going on the country- what I thought of various political and media personages and why everything was so corrupt these days.

"You know," my regular Indian driver would often say, "I have them all in my car- government ministers, journalists, civil servants; and you are better informed than nearly all of them."

"You know I had Margaret Thatcher's dresser in the car the other day? She says the poor old dear is so gaga she doesn't even realise Dennis is dead!"

"I do so enjoy our chats," he would say as he dropped me off at the offices. "Take care, my friend."

I never had the heart to admit I was only a switchboard operator. It seemed churlish.

I perfected delivery of these three phrases:

Good morning, Reuters.

Good afternoon, Reuters.

Good evening, Reuters.

This was a lot more impressive than Reuters' New York switchboard managed- i.e. "Reuters- how may I direct your call?"

At least at the London end, we held up the illusion that- just possibly- you were talking to somebody who might be actually important and was just passing the phone when it had begun to ring.

And to be fair, we had access to enormous files and folders with some quite confidential information regarding the contact details of the great and good. Had I wanted to, for example, do a poo on one of the trustees' Bentleys, I could have tracked them down to their London townhouse, Cornwall getaway, gite in France or New York penthouse.

CUNTS!

* * *

On the day that America commenced its 2003 'Shock & Awe' attack on Iraq, the switchboard became very busy indeed. An endless stream of journalists and picture editors, some unable to contain their pants-jizzing excitement, were all ringing in and out in a self-important way. It was sickening.

I had to go for a drink straight after my early shift had finished, heading to the nearest pub at St. Katherine's Docks. I had written to my MP, attended the million-strong Stop the War march, been to various meetings and yet could do nothing. Nobody in power was listening. It was a depressing experience, compounded that day by the journalists all coming alive like vampires in the aftermath.

I got a pint from the bar and took a seat outside the pub- a warm afternoon for early Spring.

Sitting a couple of tables up were a male journalist (who was writing in shorthand in a journalist's pad) and what I guess was a pictures editor, a woman flicking listlessly through photos of carnage and catastrophe on an IBM laptop, occasionally stopping to go "Oh, that's a good one" or "That one's quite nice".

She turned to the man, speaking with the unmistakable tones of the English ruling classes: "Ya, so, how's the leader column going?"

"Hunh!" the man replied. "You know how it is: bang after bang after bang. The usual jingoistic nonsense for The Sun, but David's asked me to write it, so what can I do…"

"Uh-hu. Yah. Well," she said, "See you back at the office."

As she was getting up, my fists were clenched with rage. I couldn't decide whether to leap over the table and take a swing at this odious, lying little turd whose weasel words were empowering the monstrous injustice of the attack on Iraq. But I sat there quaking with impotent rage instead, drained my drink and trudged away sadly. I walked as far as Embankment tube, crying most of the way.

* * *

Answering the phone at a financial and news conglomerate wasn't what I was really in London to do, however (if you remember, the whole 'moving to London' thing was a bit of a cock up in the first place); though the week off on full-pay after each week of nights meant I ended up trapped there longer than I should have been. To date, it remains my longest period of continued employment, only terminated after then-CEO Tom Glocer implemented a 'three strikes and you're out' policy for lateness.

As my commute went something like: walk to bus stop, bus to Clapham Junction, train to Victoria, Tube to Tower Hill, walk to office, it wasn't long before I found myself on my third strike. I resigned rather than have my contract terminated, leading to other unpleasantness that I shall return to at a later stage, like a dog returning to a pile of steaming vomit.

PSST...FANCY A BONK?
SORRY!
I SAID 'WOULD YOU LIKE A BONK'
ERM, WELL...YES PLEASE
BONK!

London, June 2003.

While my then-housemates, Orange and Lucie, were in the last stages of preparing for a month in Ibiza, in celebration of Lucie's 21st birthday, I had problems of my own. Specifically, I had no cash for the ticket.

I would trundle into work, cursing it for all I was worth, and trundle back again, drink Stella and waste time on my Mac in the evenings, getting neither richer nor poorer. I felt I was wasting my time. Any job that doesn't allow you one decent holiday a year is not worth doing.

My housemates would ask me time and again if I was going to go. I was full of 'Well, if only' and 'Still thinking about it' but the fact was they were all coining it in except for me. Orange was a qualified technician and Lucie a pole dancer in Spearmint Rhino.

How I cursed at having done an Arts degree. All I was cut out for, it seemed, was answering the phone.

* * *

Salvation arrived in the form of a text message that said

CONGRATULATIONS!!!! YOU HAVE WON 2 FREE FLIGHTS TO IBIZA!!!!!! RING THIS NUMBER TO CLAIM YOUR PRIZE 0906 **** ****. P&J promotions, SO15.

Yoinks, I thought. How lucky is that?

I tried calling the number from work but the tightasses had put a block on premium calls. So in my lunch hour I hunted down a pay phone in Tower Hamlets and listened while a recorded message d r o n e

d o n v e r y s l
o w l y a b o u t t h
e g r e a t p r i z
e I h a d w o
n a n d t h
e f u n I w
o u l d s o o
n b e h
a v i n g
o n t h
e W h i t
e I
s
l
e.

The call cost nine pounds fifty.

* * *

At home, I waited breathlessly for the postman to deliver my prize, before blacking out due to oxygen starvation.

* * *

I regained consciousness some two weeks later, when the corner of an envelope bearing my name was thrust through the door and jabbed me in the eye.

Trembling, I ripped it open to find my Official Competition Winner notification on a piece of card decorated with palm trees. Close inspection of the terms and conditions proved I was an utter fool who had been taken in by an SMS spam scam.

Two free flights would be mine if I stayed in one of three 5-star hotels on the island, the cost of which each night was more than a return flight.

Some other company was running the deal, but I still had the original text buried somewhere in my Nokia Inbox. I paged through, looking for some contact information, but all there was was P&J Promotions (not their real name), SO15.

Detective work on my part, using the internet and some Royal Mail business finder, gave me their company address. Quite by chance, the name Icstis had lodged in my mind somewhere as the regulatory body overseeing complaints about exactly this sort of thing.

"Screw me out of nine pounds fifty, will you?" I said, filling in an online form.

* * *

Not too sure what happened that July. My mates had a fantastic time in the sun, hobnobbing with Pete Tong and having debauched villa parties. I think I managed a weekend in Leicester and a couple of aimless strolls around Hyde Park.

In August, however, I got a letter from Icstis informing me they had investigated my complaint, found P&J in breach of their regulations and had fined the company five thousand pounds. They also gave me the company director's name, home address and mobile number should I wish to pursue matters with him myself.

I was amazed. For once it seemed, the system was working. It was also on my side.

* * *

That weekend, I took the train to Southampton and pissed through his letterbox.

Then I did a crap on his BMW.

September, 2014.

I fly into Surat Thani from Bangkok on one of those cheap ass airlines, whose Health & Safety booklet's exhortations to do mild exercises in the sky to avoid deep vein thrombosis are nothing more than a legal fig leaf to point to should anyone's legs explode on arrival. There's barely room to breathe, let alone make circular and up-down ankle movements and when the guy in front of me clicks his seat back as far as he can, I think "Selfish cunt!" to myself, before deciding to do the same. Behind me there's someone small and Chinese anyway who, as is typical of East Asians, has already fallen asleep.

And I think it's the lack of room that means, for once, I don't check the pocket bit in the seat back as we disembark. Which is unfortunate because I leave my iPod Classic in there, the week after they got discontinued by Apple.

I'm not to know this yet, because I'm waiting to get a coach / boat ticket to Koh Phangan via Dansak and the woman at the counter is telling me no booking no ticket. A gleaming eyed taxi guy in a pretend uniform is sizing me up for how much he can shake out of me in limousine fares for the 90 minute trip.

So I go back to the information counter who sent me over here, to complain about what's going on and suddenly all is placatory laughter and "My friend, my friend! You lucky! Have ticket for you!"

And I'm paying in a measured but stern manner, unsure whether it would be a good idea or not to suddenly explode into a fit of righteous indignation, and maybe work myself up to accuse them of being crazy water buffalo or just saying fuck you- about the extent of my Thai knowledge. But instead I settle on "Why you say to me no ticket, huh?" only repeated three or four times, each time just a little bit louder.

Disappointingly, she doesn't crumple then and there into apology. Instead she just sits moodily, looking away with a face that says she would like to kill me, or herself, or both of us.

Next thing, people are shouting at me to run to the bus, which makes a big play of gunning its engine. And, fair enough, I indeed am the last passenger to get on board, but as it doesn't actually leave for another twenty minutes I feel the engine thing is unnecessary.

And as I get on, I see why it was a good idea not to get angry back there because, unexpectedly, the bus is entirely full with Chinese holidaymakers.

The Chinese are upwardly mobile now (well, a tiny minority really- but it's a very big country, so that's still loads). They are making all kinds of journeys on the cheap transport once the exclusive preserve of backpackers, and, in the case of Britain, those pensioners enjoying the free bus passes given to them on the unlikely grounds that, as Baby Boomers, it's their right and they deserve it.

I have nothing against the Chinese; but between them and the internet, it means simply rocking up and seeing what happens is maybe no longer the case, at least in terms of transport. But they were all headed for Koh Samui in any case. And who knows what or where they ended up doing there because Chinese tourists are like winged ants in Summer: a sudden swarm of them and then they are gone.

It's about then that I realise my iPod is missing but I decide I'm more pissed off with Apple for discontinuing it than myself for leaving it. But for some reason, I can never remain angry at Apple for long, no matter how pointless their products become. I've become sadly disappointed, of course, ever since they became popular.

Night was falling as the boat left the jetty, the sunset a glorious and radiant fire of evening light refracting through billions of stratospheric aerosol geoengineering nanoparticles.

God bless science.

And once the night was fully dark, the stars were in abundance and the Milky Way was revealed for the first time in an age. I studied its magnificence- having no music to listen to. And when I got bored I watched Robot Chicken.

Arriving in Thong Sala, I found myself in a songtaew speeding towards Haad Rin.

I was with a mainly Thai bunch, all strangers to each other. One of them was periodically whooping, singing snatches of Thai songs, a few English phrases such as "Fuck you, motherfucker!" and climbing out the back to gulp draughts of the fast night air, behaviour which can't be ignored, except outwardly of course: any visible sign of reaction could make him even worse.

So a calculation has to be made- do I take this as

a) drunkenness

b) some Thai thing

c) meth head

I look at the other passengers who are all pretending this isn't happening also and follow suit.

- – -

When we arrive in Haad Rin, the place is awfully quiet: a few empty bars with lone blokes watching football on TVs that aren't even widescreen. I find somewhere to check in, deciding it's too late really to press on to Haad Yuan, the beach where I'm heading.

Haad Yuan is the next beach along, and inaccessible except by boat.

Haad Yuan had, at least the last time I came here in 2007, a really nice vibe- pleasant and friendly travellers out to have a good time with recreational pharmaceuticals, spliff and rich, thick shakes made with Thai mushrooms.

A kind of heaven then, except for the bloody mosquitos, and the sort of happy, carefree place the world used to be: back when I was young and/or before I moved to the bloody Middle East (I don't mean where I live there is actually bloody, BTW- if anything, it's merely rather dull and almost oppressively peaceful.)

I am conscious that, here and now in September 2014, I'm the same age as the first person who ever engaged me in conversation on the island, back at Paradise Bungalows in Haad Rin (Haad Yuan was uninhabited back then). He was a seeming fixture of the then fairly underground scene, called Big John. And though I say it was 'underground', even by the time of that first visit in 2001, it was more sort of 'underground, overground'. A bit like the Wombles:

- – -

Haad Rin was my first really good time in Thailand, back in 2001.

The second lot of people that I met were the Thai guys who worked there, offering me a bong hit from the next bungalow from mine.

It was a pleasant surprise after Koh Samui's dull sterility where I had got conned into prepaying for three days for some deserted beach in the middle of nowhere- whose chief characteristics had been the horror of cutting my foot when the bathroom mirror fell off the wall and then the relative joy of finding an ecstasy tablet I had forgotten about- a legacy of my going-away party a week before. And then the relative horror of imagining what might have happened had I been searched. Followed, again, by the relative joy of remembering that I hadn't been.

But Kho Phangan was a lot better.

For a while, though, I allowed Big John to be my guide and mentor, due to his deep understanding of the "omm shanty shanty" nature of Thai culture. This understanding was based on his having been here for three months and finding himself a niche knocking out MDMA and anything else in order to pay the rent. Despite not knowing any of the language beyond "sir woddy crap" and "spidery my", he impressed upon me that the Thais were an "omm shanty shanty" people who were deeply attuned to the cycles of nature, as evidenced by the enormous orgy of drug-taking and actual orgying that went on each full moon.

As for John- what can I say? At the age of 41 he had taken to wearing shells through the holes in his ears and had a way about him that seemed he was either on the verge of a breakthrough or breakdown. His hair had been dyed black on one side and bleached on the other and he was prone to bursting out into the performance poetry he had started writing. One of these went something like

What do you wanna be
Free
Like me
Or just
A wannabee?
What do you wanna do
Fool
I feel sorry for you
Living by the rules
You know you can be
free
just let go like me
And we will be mirrors
And mirrors can't see

I said I kind of liked it. It rhymed, but was unlikely to be a call to arms unless he changed the ending.

I asked what was all that stuff about mirrors. He said it just came to him when he was washing his hands and he liked it because it was only because he was looking in the mirror as he did this that there was his reflection looking back at him.

He tried to impress upon me how profound this actually was but I wasn't so sure. It seemed more like a clumsy phrase, needing rewriting for clarity.

"Well," Big John patiently explained. "I wanted to make it clearer but I got kind of stuck on the word 'mirrors'. Nothing really rhymes, except maybe 'terrors' or 'errors' and neither of them are proper rhymes. And besides, I was really looking for a happy ending."

This and a few other works he would perform on passing tourists and Thais who didn't seem know how to respond, settling on smiling or laughing politely.

The Ballad of Big John began to be bothering, to be honest. But as I was keen on MDMA and weed, and as he lived two doors down, chances are he would collar me and ask if I wanted anything. In those days I'd often answer "yes" but then he'd take cart blanche to try to monopolise my time for as long as it took me to shake him off. An attention thief, in other words.

He told me all about his previous life as a timeshare salesman in the southern Seychelles, the slurp of the surf on its soft shores a sop to his smooth sure patter, pleasing and flattering punters to sign up to repetitive breaks.

And then he had thought fuck this: this isn't what I was put on earth to do. I need to be creative and find myself. Stick seashells in my ears, dye my hair and just go native somewhere.

The poems were a stopgap while he got himself a band together, he explained. The fact that he couldn't play anything and had only ever sung in the shower was neither here nor there, he reckoned, because he'd be a natural anyway. His poems were really the lyrics for when he found the right musicians to come together and write the actual songs and perform them for him.

One Thai band were showing some interest, John told me. But they only knew No Woman, No Cry and Buffalo Soldier and John demanded that the band could only have relevance as a creative engine of new and bold material, such as

Got any weed?
Got any Veras?
Got any speed?
God, are you serious?
I got weed
I got speed
I got anything you need
I got ket
I got phet
I got LSD
You bet
I got blotters
I got poppers
Unless of course
You're coppers
In which case
The aforementioned
Was for an entertainment purpose.

I said I liked that one. It was informative for customers and had a legal caveat.

At about that time, I had been fancying another holidaymaker from Europe that I had met on Koh Samui and travelled with, but then she ended up copping off with a German idiot instead because I had been too shy and deranged and had missed the opportunity. It was grim.

So I thought I'd just make a break for it, head to Chiang Mai for a change of scene. The mushroom shakes were beginning to do my head in.

Big John was dumbfounded.

"But, but- you can't leave. Don't you understand? You're fated to stay. It's a coming together of all the tribes. Like in the Celestine Prophecy."

I had left anyway, but not before Big John gave me his farewell performance, which was a piece he had written just that day. He said it wasn't about me.

So
Just go
But just know
You could grow
If only though
You could see
Like me
Then you could be free
Of the errors of your ways
In the mirrors of your maze
In the middle of your days
In the muddle of your ways
You have yet
To get
Free
You have yet
To be
Like me

Oh no
I don't think so
You have
A long way to go.

He explained he had written it about the manager at the timeshare office back in the Seychelles, but I wasn't so sure.

- – -

Two months later, after I had done a TEFL course in Phuket, I went back to Koh Phangan.

I returned to the Paradise Bungalows but had to stay in a different bungalow.

Times had changed.

I asked the Thai bong smokers what had happened to Big John- I hadn't seen him around.

"He not Big John no more. He big mother fucker. He go away. He owe money. He not tell truth. He bad man!"

They wouldn't be more specific.

The next day, I bumped into him.

"Hello, Rick." He said. "Great to see a friendly face around here."

He filled me in on his moving to a cheap omm shanty shanty hut on the other beach and how the Paradise Bungalows lot were all fucking liars who didn't know what they were talking about.

It was true, he conceded, that his visa had expired and he didn't know how he could renew it as nearly all his timeshare savings were gone. I asked if he could afford a TEFL course. He said he wasn't put here to be a teacher- he was a creative artist:

I was born to create
I was made to make
I don't teach, bitch
I reach, bitch
And when I see you
When I am rich
I will definitely pay you
I'm telling you,
Trust me
Omm shanty shanty
Omm shanty shanty

ThIs he performed as a verbal IOU in lieu of rent to his omm shanty shanty landlord who promptly threw him out, Big John protesting all the time "But you can't DO that! You can't actually DO that!"

After that, he was strangely never seen again and nobody ever knew what happened to him, at least among the tourists.

If you asked the Thais they'd go all quiet in a way that made you wish you'd never asked.

250 millilitres...
half a gallon...
98 cubic feet...
Well, that
speaks
volumes
makeyourselfuncomfortable.net

Acknowledgements

Thanks to Rob H. Goering who wrote the words for some of the comic strips. Blame him.

Thanks go to everyone else who gave feedback on the work. You know who you are.

MYU

makeyourselfuncomfortable.net